Acknowledgments

To Joseph and Elizabeth

Thank you

Table of Contents

Introduction   pp

Chapter One-Smoking Generally   **15**
Smoking generally   15
Smoking in pregnancy   16
Points to consider   19
Smoking in Children and teens   20

Chapter Two-What's in a smoke?   **23**
Nicotine.   23
Carbon-monoxide   24
Tar   24
Arsenic   24
Hydrogen Cyanide   24
Ammonia   25
Nitrogen-dioxide.   25
Acrolein   25
Formaldehyde   25
Naphthylamine and Nitrosamines   25
Difference between tobacco and cigarettes   25
Electronic or E-Cigarettes   26
Are E-cigarettes safe to use?   27
Do E-cigarettes help people quit smoking?   27

Chapter Three-Why do people smoke?   **29**

Addiction   29

Habit   30

Peer pressure   31

Parental Influence   31

To rebel or break rules   32

To relieve stress   32

Boredom   33

To relax   33

To lose weight   33

To socialise   34

Mental Illness   35

Advertising   35

Lack of Awareness   36

Other reasons   36

Chapter Four-Nicotine Addiction   **39**

Addiction generally   39

Nicotine dependence   41

Cravings and withdrawal pangs   41

Risk factors for prevalence of addiction   42

Chapter Five-Why Give Up Smoking?   **43**

Health   43

To protect your loved ones and pets   44

To save money   45

Longevity   46

Common reasons smokers give to quit smoking   46

Chapter Six-The Stop Smoking Plan   **49**

The stages of change when quitting smoking   49

Pre-contemplation   49

Contemplation   50

Preparation   50

Action   50

Maintenance   51

Relapse   51

Cognitive Dissonance in smoking   52

Self-efficacy in quitting smoking   53

Will-power in quitting smoking   54

Motivation in the process of quitting smoking   55

The smoke free plan or diary   57

Chapter Seven-Smoking and the Mind   **61**

The brainwashed mind   63

The fearful mind   65

Points to consider   66

Chapter Eight-Stop Smoking Therapies   **67**

Hypnotherapy   67

The Hypnotherapy session   69

Self-hypnosis script recording   69

Quit Smoking Script 1   71

Quit smoking script 2   75

Cognitive Behavioural Therapy for quitting smoking   79

Changing smoking thinking patterns   80

CBT technique for stop smoking   80

Counselling: The Motivational Interview 82

Positive Thinking and Affirmations in quit smoking 86

Helpful quit smoking affirmations 87

Deep Breathing Technique in stop smoking 88

Breathing Exercise 89

Progressive Muscle Relaxation(PMR) 89

Progressive Muscle Relaxation technique 90

Acupuncture in the quit smoking process 91

Chapter Nine-Nicotine Replacement Therapy (NRT) **93**

NRT generally 93

The Nicotine Patch 95

Nicotine Chewing Gum 95

Nicotine Nasal Spray 96

Inhaler 97

Nicotine Mouth Spray 98

Nicotine Lozenges 98

Chapter Ten-Stop-Smoking Medicines **101**

Zyban (Buplopion) 101

Side effects of Zyban 102

Champix (Varenicline) 102

Side effects 103

Chapter Eleven-A Review of Lifestyle When Quitting **105**
Smoking

Generally 105

A healthy diet 105

Exercise   107

Exercise options   107

Go to bed early   108

Change your daily routine   109

Avoid smokers   109

Remove all reminders of smoking   109

Chapter Twelve-Staying On Track   **110**

General advice and support   110

** **

Book references

Resources

Index

Introduction

Studies show that not many people really understand the specific health risks of tobacco use. Among smokers who are aware of the dangers of smoking most want to quit but are deep into addiction. Most smokers believe that they choose to smoke, every time they light up a cigarette they think that they are doing it out of personal choice, which is not true. Likewise, a high number of smokers are mystified as to why they continue with a habit that causes them harm, a feeling that leaves them hopeless. In order to overcome this feeling they make up excuses in an attempt to explain why they are putting their health and well-being at risk.

The truth is that many people who smoke do not enjoy smoking but they do it because they are addicted. Many say that if they had a choice they wouldn't be smoking in the first place as they feel guilty and disgusted that they even smoke. So why do they carry on smoking? Is it because they are deep in the chains of addiction, is it because the habit is no longer controllable, or is it the brainwashing that is sabotaging their ability to stop smoking?

Realistically when you are addicted to the nicotine in cigarettes, your power to choose is completely removed from you. And so the battle continues in the smoker's mind, desperately trying to regain control amid searching for excuses to continue smoking and convincing themselves that they will quit whenever they want to, meanwhile getting even more addicted. In reality smokers who put their hands up and accept that they have a problem and need help, will make the decision to quit easier and quicker than those in denial.

If you want to change your habits you have to recognize and understand the reason why you smoke, focus on the benefits that you gain by stopping smoking and avoid dwelling on the negatives of giving up. There are going to be bad days but to be successful in your attempts you have to learn how to respond to these challenges by learning from them.

Whether you are an addicted smoker or a habitual smoker you can stop smoking. I guess you have picked this book because you want to kick the habit, it may be your first, second, third attempt or more, it doesn't matter. What matters is that you have put yourself back in charge again, there is no one size fits all when it comes to stopping smoking, you have to keep trying until you find a method that works for you. What I'm sure of is that each time you try, you give yourself the best chance of giving up smoking for good. Any smoker can give up smoking easily and permanently as long as they accept that they have a problem.

Many people have given up smoking which is evidence that you can too if you are willing to put in the hard work. Also remember that you have to take responsibility for your thoughts, feelings and behaviours towards smoking, accept that you made the choice to smoke, (you didn't have to but you did), no one can make you smoke without your permission and don't make excuses and blame others and circumstances for your smoking because when you blame other people you will be shifting the responsibility on to others hence blocking your chances of successfully quitting. Accepting that you're the creator of your smoking habit will power your motivation to turn your life around and become a non-smoker.

The purpose of this book is to simply guide you to use the powers that you already possess within you to quit smoking and become a non-smoker for good. People can and do recover from smoking addiction either by self-help therapy, psychological therapy, medical help or through a mixture of these. This book is simple, short and to the point so that you find it easy to digest the information and the diverse techniques in it.

Chapter 1, 2 and 3 explore smoking facts, what's in a smoke and the main reasons why people smoke.

Chapters 4,5 and 6 explore addiction and its roots, how smoking damages health and the benefits of giving up smoking as well as the stop smoking plan.

Chapters 7,8 and 9 detail how smoking affects the mind and how therapies like hypnotherapy, Cognitive Behavioural Therapy, Nicotine Replacement therapy, and others can help in the smoking cessation process.

Chapters 10, 11 and 12 look further into stop smoking medications and how they can help with quit smoking. These chapters also explore lifestyle review such as eating a balanced diet, exercise and a change in routine. They also examine a range of various ways on how to stay on track and avoid a relapse.

Life choices-Decisions

It's part of human nature to consciously or subconsciously fall into behaviours and habits on a daily basis, some of which are positive and others negative, for example smoking, gambling, alcoholism and drug use the list goes on. This doesn't mean that we are weak or less human, in fact it emphasises that we are human after all capable of falling at life's many hurdles but also capable of rising from challenges wiser and stronger, hence making better choices. In life we make our choices and therefore in the process we create the people we become by those choices. We must therefore strive to make the right ones and if for any reason we don't we do our best to learn from the wrong ones and correct them. The power of choice is significant and it's important to reflect on the lessons learnt and also grow from the decisions we make. Unfortunately very often we are fearful of our judgement wishing that someone would come along and make the decisions for us because the burden of making them feels so heavy, so we choose not to do anything and bury our heads in the sand even when we know that we desperately need to take the plunge, especially with a health-threatening habit like smoking. But for sure what I understand about smoking is that you will be amazed at how many benefits will come from quitting and perhaps your only regret will be that you didn't quit sooner. Once you make that decision to quit don't look back. Tell yourself that you are a non-smoker and behave like one. Show respect to your body and treat it well, as your body is worthy of respect and proper care for it to function at its full capacity.

To take this further;

- o Prepare yourself for the decision you are going to make. In this case stop smoking. Equip yourself with all the information and facts about smoking
- o Assess the benefits and outcomes i.e. what the decision to quit means to you and what changes you need to make to see your goals through.
- o Follow through with this decision. Once you decide to stop smoking don't be fearful and doubtful. Have belief in yourself and don't look back. Take action NOW.

Remember that the power of choice is yours. If you change out of fear, doubt or to please others, your stop smoking journey will lack substance and your decision may result in regret.

Likewise if you don't make the decision nothing will happen. The only way we learn is by doing. The strongest principle of growth lies in human choice so use it wisely!

**

Chapter One

Smoking Generally

According to the World Health Organisation

- Smoking kills up to half of its users.
- Tobacco continues to be the substance causing the maximum health damage globally.
- Tobacco kills around 6 million people each year. More than 5 million of those deaths are a result of direct tobacco use while more than 600,000 are the result of non-smokers being exposed to second hand smoke.

Tobacco smoking is the highest single cause of illness and premature death in the United Kingdom, killing over 120,000 people every year. Smoking is dangerous and it kills. A good number of smokers know this but they still carry on smoking. Fortunately, unlike food, sleep and exercise, the body doesn't need cigarettes, smoking is not a human need which should realistically make it easy for a smoker to quit. When you smoke you have a lot at stake. Smokers will often continue to smoke or struggle to give up for a number of reasons, but in many cases it's the fact that they give themselves plenty of excuses to carry on smoking and these are some of them.

- I am not addicted to smoking, I know I can stop any time I want to.
- I only smoke a few so no harm done.
- I will stop smoking when I feel better.
- I will put on weight if I stop smoking.
- When I fall pregnant I will stop.
- I will stop after I've given birth
- I will have my last packet then stop.
- I only smoke in social situations.
- Smoking relaxes and calms me down.
- Smoking reduces my stress.
- Smoking is my only treat.
- I only smoke when I drink.
- I smoke to pass time.
- It's only cigarettes not drugs.
- The damage is already done so what's point?
- I know of smokers who have lived longer.
- I will stop when I'm 20, 30, 40, 50 and so forth.
- I feel confident and happier after I smoke.
- I am still healthy and strong.
- Smoking comforts me.

Smoking in pregnancy

Many women smoke while they are pregnant and some of them have genuinely tried to quit smoking but to no avail. if you are reading this and thinking this applies to me, I'm hoping that the well-being of your baby will be the trigger that you need to quit for good, however tough it is when cravings strike. Sadly the further you smoke into pregnancy the greater the risk of complications for you and your baby. Smoking does not only damage the health of the smoker, but it also puts the life of the unborn baby at risk. There are 4000 chemicals in a cigarette, all these toxins are carried through your blood stream directly to your baby via the umbilical cord and placenta which are the only sources of nutrients and oxygen for your baby.

Babies and children whose mothers smoke during pregnancy are more likely to develop asthma, allergies, lung infections, heart defects, respiratory problems as well as Sudden Infant Death Syndrome(SIDS) or cot death. Babies of smoking mothers are commonly born with under-developed bodies which means that their lungs may also be weak and therefore not able to work on their own without the use of a respirator.

Nevertheless if you stop smoking during the first half of your pregnancy your baby will be likely to have a healthy birth weight so it's never too late. Giving up smoking to protect your baby from the abrasive effects of smoking will not only be one of the best decisions you'll ever make, but you will also be ensuring that you are giving your baby the best possible start in life. It is always safer to give up smoking a few months before trying for a baby, but having said that there are many women who conceive unexpectedly. If this happens stop smoking completely. For those who are trying to conceive but are still smoking, smoking will make it harder for you to conceive and reduces your chances of IVF success as well. In men trying to conceive, it's important to understand that smoking lowers your sperm count and affect its quality too.

Sadly in the those unfortunate cases where expectant mothers smoke throughout pregnancy and after giving birth, it is still advisable to stop smoking once your baby is born in view of the fact that this is the only single way of protecting you and your baby from the harmful effects of smoking. However if you're still struggling to quit smoking don't stop breastfeeding your baby because the breast milk is crucial in protecting your baby from infections and also providing nutrients that can't possibly be found in formula milk but bear in mind that smoking more than ten cigarettes a day decreases breast milk production.

To add to this, parents who are smokers expose their children to the health risks of smoking. When exposed to smoke a non-smoker's risk of lung cancer rises to 24% and their risk of heart disease goes up to 25%. This is more so with children who are exposed to cigarette smoke who can also develop asthma. The earlier you quit the better, do not try and convince yourself that smoking less cigarettes is less harmful to yourself and everyone else, there's no safe level of smoking. Even a couple of cigarettes are enough to deliver the toxic nicotine to damage your health and your children's. An even better reason for a parent to quit smoking.

The benefits of quitting smoking in pregnancy are innumerable for you and your baby. You will both experience the effects immediately.

For instance:

- Your baby will be less likely to be born underweight, which is a common problem in babies of women who smoke during pregnancy.
- The risk of cot death or SIDS (Sudden Infant Death) will be reduced.
- You will reduce the risk of still birth.
- Your baby will be less likely to be born prematurely.
- The risk of complications in pregnancy and birth will be averted.
- Additionally you will have a better chance of having a healthier pregnancy and baby.

Points to consider

- Smoking in pregnancy is harmful to you and your baby
- If your partner smokes they should consider stopping smoking or at least not smoke around you
- Protect yourself and your baby from other smokers, passive smoke is equally harmful
- You should aim to stop smoking completely when you fall pregnant
- If you or your partner can't stop smoking its important not to share a bed with your baby

- Get rid of all your smoking reminders
- Get help, advice and support for smoking if you are struggling to quit, discuss any stop smoking therapies with your doctor

Smoking in children and teens

According to Cancer Research UK 200,000 children start smoking every year from the ages 11-15 meaning that 570 children start smoking everyday which is a staggering and shocking number of children taking up smoking in one single day! Many children will start smoking and even carry on for a while without the knowledge of their parents, often smoking away from home, in a secret place, taking preventative measures to ensure their clothes don't pick up any smoke odour, getting their friends to get their cigarette supplies or steal from their parents if they are smokers and so forth. Once a child is hooked on smoking they will go to any length to keep their nicotine starvation at arm's length. However there are certain signs that parents can look out for which may suggest that their child is smoking;

- Smoke odour on their clothes
- They may display a range of emotions like being anxious, moody stressed, agitated.
- Coughing and suffering from more coughs
- Stained teeth, hands and nails
- Bad breath
- Shortness of breath
- Secretiveness, sneakiness or even fidgety

Studies show that parents who smoke in front of their children may do more harm than they realize. Besides the obvious dangers of exposing second hand smoke and its hazardous risks you may also not realize that you are indirectly introducing smoking into their lives and also providing them with easy access to cigarettes. Children furthermore tend to look up to their parents as role models so there is danger that your children may want to take up smoking themselves and consequently acquiring childhood taste for nicotine and getting hooked. The thing is once they've started it will be difficult for parents who smoke to convince them to give up whilst carrying on smoking themselves.

Sometimes children think that smoking is normal and it's something that's cool to do because they see their parents and other adults doing it. This is why quitting smoking yourself first will be the best possible start in such a scenario which means that you will be more believable when trying to persuade your child to quit. Not only will they take you more serious but they will also have respect for you. Nevertheless whatever the outcome its important to talk to your child and make them understand the dangers of smoking.

Points to consider

- For you to quit smoking and set a good example

- Find out why your child started smoking and what they find appealing about smoking and locate ways to support them.
- Talk to them without threatening them or coming across as judgemental about the dangers of smoking and the health risks associated with it.
- Make your home a smoke free zone and get rid of anything to do with smoking so there's no temptations for your child.
- If they have smoking friends who are pressuring them into smoking encourage them to spend time with friends who don't smoke. Smokers have a habit of resenting other people who are quitting so arm your child with this information so they know what to expect and how to handle such situations.
- If you have tried everything and nothing seems to be stopping your child from smoking seek professional help as it can be difficult to stop once the nicotine addiction has kicked in, especially at a young age.

**

Chapter Two

What is in a Smoke?

It is estimated that there are over 4000 chemicals in cigarettes. I've come across many people who smoke but don't know what is in a cigarette and the numerous health risks that they expose themselves to. If you are serious about stopping smoking, the first step you should take is to address reality and start educating yourself about the contents of a cigarette and the effects of each of those contents to your health and the grave risks that smoking presents. Many smokers see the warnings on cigarette packs like "Smoking Kills", " Smoking clogs the arteries and causes heart attacks and strokes" and more warnings on television and other media outlets but they still choose to carry on smoking either because they are in the depths of addiction and denial or because they don't know the extent to which smoking puts their health at risk.

The major contents in a cigarette are nicotine, carbon-monoxide and tar.

Nicotine- Nicotine is a chemical compound found in tobacco, it is a poisonous substance that is responsible for causing cravings, during smoking. Nicotine is absorbed through the wall lining of the small air sacs in the lungs where it's quickly absorbed into the bloodstream. When sniffed or chewed, nicotine is absorbed through the mucous membranes of the nose or mouth. People who smoke regularly expose their bodies to this substance on a daily basis. Nicotine causes low blood pressure, nausea, vomiting, pain, confusion and also contributes to heart disease.

Carbon-monoxide(CO)- This is a toxic odourless, colourless, tasteless gas that if inhaled is fatal. This chemical starves the body of oxygen, its present in all tobacco smoke and can cause shortness of breath, contribute to build up of fat in artery walls and also lead to heart disease and low birth weight in babies of expectant mothers who smoke during pregnancy.

Tar- Is a sticky black toxic chemical residual left behind from burning cigarettes containing hundreds of chemicals which are hazardous. Tar in cigarette smoke paralyzes the cilia in the lungs and contributes to lung diseases such as emphysema, chronic bronchitis and lung cancer.

Other contents are;

Arsenic- is a poisonous chemical often used in herbicides and pesticides used to control various pests for example rats, mice, ticks. One of the channels where people are exposed to heightened levels of arsenic is through tobacco smoking.

Hydrogen Cyanide–An extremely poisonous warfare chemical used commercially for many things including mining, fumigation, electro-planting and more. It is potentially lethal to humans.

Ammonia-A chemical compound used in the manufacture of fertilizers, explosives and cleaning fluids which is poisonous if inhaled. It is commonly found in many household cleaning products.

Nitrogen-dioxide- this is also a chemical compound used in manufacturing of nitric acid, chemical explosives and flour bleaching agent. If inhaled nitrogen-dioxide inflames the lining of the lungs, it may cause respiratory problems and also reduce immunity to lung infections.

Acrolein-Is a colourless or yellow liquid that is toxic and commonly used in the manufacturing of acrylic acid.

Formaldehyde-Another venomous colourless, flammable strong smelling chemical used in industrial and manufacturing of numerous household products.

Naphthylamine-and Nitrosamines – Are both harmful chemicals used in the manufacturing of numerous products.

Difference between tobacco and cigarettes

Many people don't understand the difference between cigarettes and tobacco; tobacco is a plant most commonly grown for its leaves in warm climates, its leaves are dried and fermented before being added into tobacco products. Tobacco can be smoked in a cigarette, pipe, or cigar although some people chew it or sniff it through their noses. A large proportion of people don't know that tobacco contains nicotine. Nicotine is a natural product of tobacco and its botanical name is "nicotiana tabacum" it is highly addictive this is why people who smoke it find it impossible to quit. It is the nicotine component which makes tobacco a hugely popular substance worldwide. Together with nicotine there are other potentially harmful chemicals found in tobacco or generated by burning it.

Cigarettes are finely cut tobacco leaves wrapped in paper for smoking. Cigarettes are one of the most smoked tobacco products. When a cigarette is burnt it releases over 5000 different poisonous chemicals.

It's important to note that both tobacco and cigarettes are harmful to your health.

Electronic or E-Cigarettes

A lot has been said about e-cigarettes through books, newspapers, magazines, internet, on television adverts and bill boards. Everywhere you look is some kind of information about them, but the truth is that there isn't enough scientific evidence to clarify all that's being said about them.

To begin with, an e-cigarette is a device that allows nicotine inhalation without most of the harmful effects of smoking. When a person smokes a tobacco cigarette, smoke is inhaled into the lungs and then exhaled, whereas if they are smoking an e-cigarette, the vapour is released into the air only when the smoker inhales. There is no smoke because there is no burning involved. Using e-cigarettes is often called vaping. E-cigarettes are battery operated, usually rechargeable devices. As the user inhales, the battery heats up the liquid inside the cartridge and produces a vapour which delivers a hit of nicotine.

Are E-cigarettes safe to use?

Although E-cigarettes don't contain carbon-monoxide, tar and other toxic substances that are found in tobacco cigarettes, they are not risk free. However based on current evidence they carry a fraction of the risk of cigarettes. E-cigarettes contain nicotine and vapour can contain prospective harmful chemicals. They are still new, therefore there's not enough evidence yet about their safety which will become evident with the passage of time.

Do E-cigarettes help people quit smoking?

Evidence shows that E-cigarettes can help people quit smoking with similar results as NRT. However, to properly control your cravings, you will have to use your E-cigarettes frequently. Actually I have heard numerous people say that they succeeded in quitting smoking using E-cigarettes mainly because it reduced the amount of nicotine levels. This then allowed them to get less nicotine each time they smoked and this way they were able to slowly reduce their addiction to nicotine, thereafter breaking their smoking habits. Finally, if you use E-cigarettes less frequently then your chances of quitting will be minimal.

Chapter Three

Why Do People Smoke?

When you ask smokers why they smoke you will be presented with a range of reasons but the common ones I've come across are;

Addiction

Addiction is both what happens when you use the substance and when you don't use it. An addiction to cigarettes will lead to a smoker to go to extreme lengths to smoke. As we have discussed, this addiction is caused by nicotine, a chemical compound that is present in the tobacco. Nicotine is one of the most addictive substances on the planet and one of the hardest addiction to break. But nevertheless it is breakable. Smokers will always find it easy to say that they have a habit of smoking than saying that they are addicted . This is because saying that they have a habit makes them think that they have the power to give up any time or that they are in control, whereas saying that they are addicted, puts them in a position of no control at all which is scary to say the least.

For this reason you will rarely find a smoker who admits that he or she is addicted. For the addicted smoker, admitting that you're addicted shouldn't be something to be ashamed of. If you are addicted to cigarettes and admit to needing help, this is an impressive first step to successfully quitting smoking.

Habit

As well as being an addiction, smoking can also be a habit. Habits are not addictions but bad habits share traits of addictive behaviours, and bad habits like smoking can become addictions which eventually culminate in destructive and exceedingly difficult to control patterns. The smoking habit is reinforced by the routines, times, places, activities, rituals and people you associate smoking with. Because habits are repetitive, they eventually enter your subconscious mind where they are stored and become part of you. Hence, once a habit is stored there , you won't have to think too much about it, you will just do it automatically. To further illustrate this, driving a car is a programmed habit, you can drive it whilst thinking about other things but still performing all the right manoeuvres. The smoking habit is the same. It will be something you do automatically without giving too much thought.

Fortunately by re-programming your mind, good habits can be developed and bad habits can be broken. Common smoking habits include; lighting up a cigarette automatically without thinking whether you want one or not, seeing someone light up or smoking, accepting a cigarette that someone has offered, lighting up after finishing a meal, watching television, after or with a cup of tea/coffee, smoking while answering the phone, lighting up at the bus stop, train station, in the car, at the pub, even in your garden at home.

Peer pressure

Most people take up smoking when they're in their teens, mainly due to peer pressure and their desire to fit in with the crowd, to look cool, to experience or copy famous people who they idolise who smoke. Research shows that teens are more likely to get hooked on cigarettes if their friends smoke and if they feel alienated from school. But unfortunately because nicotine in the cigarettes is highly addictive they get addicted and find it difficult to give up and accordingly continue to smoke into their adulthood.

Parental influence

It is very well documented that children of parents who smoke are twice as likely to begin smoking as well. This may be due to numerous factors but among them is that because these children are around tobacco they are exposed to second hand smoke which may result in nicotine addiction early on. Another factor is the availability of cigarettes at home, which makes it easy for children to acquire cigarettes. On top of that children emulate their parents and, sad to say, if their parents smoke they are also more likely to smoke. Studies show that teens are strongly influenced by parental smoking and that attitudes, behaviours and beliefs towards smoking are learned through modelling. Therefore children and teens who observe their parents smoking absorb their parents' smoking experiences and develop expectations for themselves.

To rebel or break rules

A vast majority of teenagers start smoking because they simply enjoy breaking the rules and find it exciting to feel as though they are in control and can do whatever they want. And because teens are quite difficult anyway there is always this massive disconnect between what their parents say and what the teenagers want. Their yearning for freedom eventually turns into a rebellious attitude and behaviours smoking being one of these behaviours. Teenagers view smoking as a great way to challenge authority and build a sense of self, proving to their parents that they have the authority to make their own choices.

To relieve stress

A vast number of people smoke to escape their worries, troubles and anxieties that cause their stress. Since stress is part of life, relying on cigarettes to combat it is a hazardous way which often contributes to long-time smoking and inability to quit. Although smokers often report that smoking relieves their stress temporarily, they also note that if they didn't smoke they often feel even more stressed. This becomes a cycle as they feel agitated and moody between cigarettes and so when they smoke again they feel better and the pattern continues. Moreover there are better and more healthy ways to relieve stress than smoking.

Boredom

Some people smoke because they are bored of what they are doing or have nothing to do to pass their time. However, the contrast here is that when you smoke you concentrate on only one thing which is smoking and thinking, consequently heightening your boredom because smoking pins you down in one place and all you do is think and smoke even more and as soon as you finish the cigarette your boredom returns and you light up another one.

To relax

Some smokers believe that smoking relaxes them to a certain degree. Nicotine stimulates the brain to release dopamine, a hormone linked with pleasurable feelings. The smoker feels relaxed but only temporarily because as the nicotine wears off so does the heightened feelings of pleasure or relaxation. To be able to relax again they light another cigarette thus developing a regular smoking pattern.

To lose weight

Weight loss is a genuine concern for people who want to give up smoking as smokers tend to use cigarettes to overcome hunger, and when the option is no longer available, they will switch to eating, thus putting on weight. A point to note is that smoking doesn't necessarily help to lose weight, what happens is that when you smoke your taste buds become damaged which renders them less sensitive and as a result you eat less. Additionally nicotine suppresses your appetite and speeds up your metabolism, leading to weight loss.

When a smoker stops smoking, their taste buds are restored to normal and because they have no nicotine in their blood stream, their appetite returns too. Research shows that the average person who stops smoking gains about 4 kilograms mainly by snacking. Some people use food as a substitute for cigarettes or use it as a means to suppress their emotions which is also termed emotional eating. Other quitters will struggle with what to do with their hands as they are so used to holding a cigarette, and will start to pick on food.

However not everyone puts on weight when they quit smoking, and it is important that if you're quitting smoking to eat and maintain a healthy and balanced diet and exercise regularly to sustain you in the stop smoking process. This will not only help you to lose weight but also help your body cope with withdrawal symptoms from nicotine. I can't emphasise enough that the health benefits of quitting smoking heavily outweigh those of carrying on smoking to lose weight. A bit of weight is a very small price to pay. Many non-smokers manage their weight successfully without smoking. Smokers can do the same!

To socialise

Smoking can also be a social habit whereby smokers smoke occasionally or in the company of other smokers. Many smokers classify themselves as social smokers when they are actually in denial of their smoking habit and their addiction to nicotine. They mask this, terming themselves social smokers when they are actually full-blown smokers. Literally genuine social smokers often don't smoke alone, they limit their smoking to weekends and are not addicted to nicotine. This is not to say that social smoking is safe, the cigarettes they smoke still contains the same harmful chemicals that are harmful to health.

Mental illness

The association between smoking and mental health conditions is a strong one, meaning that smoking prevalence amongst mental health sufferers is higher than in the general population. The most common explanation for this is that mental health sufferers use smoking to alleviate the symptoms of their illnesses.

Advertising

Exposure to cigarette advertising, especially through movies and magazines, contributes to smoking, particularly in adolescents who have never smoked before or those who have minimal levels of smoking. Advertisers have always targeted teenagers because most smokers take up smoking in their teens anyway. They understand well that this age group is all about the image and for this reason highly susceptible to marketing that promises coolness, being more popular, independent and looking mature. Unfortunately for the tobacco industry to make copious amounts of money means that their targets are primarily focused on addiction as early on in the teen years as possible. That is why so many teenagers and young adults are smoking these days and don't even know why they continue to do it.

Lack of awareness

While many smokers are aware of the damage smoking does to their health and well-being there are a large number who are unaware or misinformed about the many issues associated with smoking in particular the illnesses that smoking causes and the fact that these illnesses cost a lot of money to treat. Worse still is the lack of realisation that half of smokers die early from their smoking habit.

Other reasons for smoking are;

- To help with concentration
- They enjoy smoking
- To experience what smoking feels like
- Adventure
- A family habit where smoking is accepted and celebrated
- To look cool
- To be deal with emotions
- The easy availability of cigarettes .

In summary, addiction to nicotine is the major reason why people smoke. Nicotine is one of the most addictive substances   there is, making smokers want to smoke more and more to feed their addiction, no matter how grim the consequences.

**

Chapter Four

Nicotine Addiction

Addiction is defined by The World Health Organisation (WHO) as "repeated use of a psychoactive substance or substances to the extent that the user is;

- Periodically or chronically intoxicated
- Showing a compulsion to take the substance
- Has difficulty in stopping or reducing substance use
- Exhibiting determination to obtain psychoactive substances by any means
- Tolerance is prominent and a withdrawal syndrome frequently occurs when substance use is interrupted

Similarly, the Royal College of Physicians lists the following criteria for addiction;

- A strong desire to take the drug or substance
- Substance is taken in large amounts for longer than intended
- Difficulty in controlling use
- A lot of time spent in obtaining, using or recovering from the effects of the substance

- A higher priority is given to substance use than to other activities and obligations
- Continued use despite harmful consequences
- Tolerance
- Withdrawal

As we have seen, Nicotine is a poisonous and highly addictive chemical compound that is present in cigarettes. It acts as a stimulant even if taken in small doses. Nicotine has a complex series of actions, both stimulating and relaxing, it stimulates the adrenal glands to release adrenaline and cortisol, raising blood pressure and heart rate. The addictive effect of nicotine is linked to its ability to release dopamine a chemical that is associated with feelings of pleasure, that is why smokers use it to reduce stress, anxiety and as a stimulant for relaxation. But as time goes on, the smoker develops tolerance to the extent that they will need larger doses of nicotine to induce the feelings of pleasure, inevitably falling into addiction.

Tolerance to nicotine develops quickly, which may be why most smokers say that the first cigarette of the day is the most enjoyable. This may be due to the fact that that first cigarette relieves the withdrawal symptoms caused by nicotine levels in the body diminishing overnight. Realistically smokers should view nicotine as a monster that deprives them of their right to be healthy mentally, physically and emotionally.

The signs of nicotine dependence are;

- Inability to stop smoking with many failed attempts to stop.
- Experiencing withdrawal symptoms when you try to stop smoking such as irritability, difficulty concentrating, restlessness, anxiety, depression, anger, low moods, sleep problems, reduced or increased appetite, agitation, hopelessness.
- Strong cravings
- You carry on smoking despite knowing the health and financial implications that smoking is exposing you to.
- Spending a lot of time obtaining nicotine.
- You would rather smoke than engage in social activities or hobbies as smoking becomes your main priority taking up all your time.

Cravings and withdrawal pangs

When you smoke you become addicted to nicotine in the cigarettes, it's what gives you the urge to smoke, that is why when you go for a long period of time without smoking you will experience and feel urges to smoke. For those who are in the process of quitting smoking, the nicotine in your blood stream will drop because you are not smoking anymore, this is when the use of nicotine substitutes like patches, gums, sprays and others are useful to feed off the nicotine hunger. Nicotine does not stay in the body for long. During the withdrawal period you are also likely to experience nicotine withdrawal symptoms like mood swings, anxiety, cravings, difficulty concentrating, aggression, irritability, sleep difficulties, hunger, weight gain, restlessness, agitation.

It is however important to stress that the withdrawal symptoms of nicotine do not cause any physical pain but are equally powerful. As we have seen, cigarettes are not a necessity like food, you can survive without them if you hang in there and be able to let the pangs pass, soon the nicotine will leave your body, so will your symptoms. Although it depends on individuals, in most cases symptoms last from one to four weeks, getting worse for a while and then getting better. What you have to remember is that you are not your addiction, you are stronger than it and absolutely capable of beating it.

Risk factors for prevalence of addiction

- Coming from a poor background
- Experience of abuse
- Children whose parents smoke are more likely to smoke than children of non-smokers
- Difficulties and instability in the family unit
- Smoking as a teenager
- Children in the company of those who smoke
- Lack of or little information on smoking facts
- Influence from media
- Celebrity influence on young people

**

Chapter Five

Why Give Up Smoking?

---

1. Health

Quitting smoking is going to be a hard task but once you make the decision to give up, it will be among the best decisions you've made in your life. You won't regret it because you will experience dramatic positive changes in your life, some of which will be immediate and others long-term.

When you smoke you put your health at risk as smoking is one of the biggest causes of preventable death and illness in the UK. It is also estimated that the yearly global death toll is 6 million! Smoking harms nearly every organ in the body and significantly reduces both quality of life and life expectancy.

Tobacco smoke is hugely harmful to your health as it affects the central nervous system, respiratory system, cardiovascular system, digestive system, reproductive system, causing numerous serious illnesses many of which are fatal while others can cause irreversible long-term damage to your health. Smoking related illness include;

- Cancers- Lung, mouth, lips, throat, oesophagus, liver, bladder, pancreas, bowels, ovary, cervix, stomach, kidney, larynx.

- Respiratory- Chronic Obstructive Pulmonary Disease(COPD) which incorporates bronchitis and emphysema, pneumonia.
- Circulatory- Coronary Heart Disease, Heart attack, stroke, Peripheral Vascular Disease, Cerebrovascular Disease
- Diabetes
- Asthma
- In pregnancy it causes - Miscarriage, premature birth, still birth, a low birth weight baby
- Blindness and cataracts and Age related Macular Degeneration
- Premature ageing
- Fertility problems
- Rheumatoid arthritis

It's never too late to kick the habit of smoking, once you stop smoking your general health will improve as your body begins to recover.

2. To protect your loved ones and pets

Smoking not only harms you, but also the ones you love for instance your partner if they don't smoke, your children, extended family and your pets if you own any. Some people bizarrely think that pets are immune from cigarette smoke which is not true, vets will tell you that at post mortem they can easily tell the pets of a smoker from those of a non-smoker. In addition, new research shows that animals exposed to second-hand smoke go on to develop a host of illnesses including cancer and cell damage. Further, second-hand smoke is the main way smoking harms non-smokers. When a non-smoker is around a person who smokes, they breathe in the smoke that comes from the cigarette as well as the smoke breathed out by the smoker. That being the case second-hand smoke is dangerous to anyone who breathes it in, as even when breathed in for a short time it can still harm your body. Second-hand smoke is especially harmful to babies, children and expectant mothers.

Over time, second-hand smoke has been linked to serious illnesses in non-smokers like lung cancer, heart disease, breathing problems and many more. So quitting smoking will be of great benefit to the family of a smoker, besides setting a good example to your children and, as highlighted before it's very common for children of smokers to take up smoking themselves because of what they see as an acceptable habit and also because of the availability of cigarettes at home. Besides when you quit smoking you will be able to spend the time you used to smoke as quality time with your family and friends (which is another bonus)!

3. To save money
Think what else you can do with the money saved from buying cigarettes! Stopping smoking will save you a great deal of money. The truth is that smoking is an expensive habit. On average most people who quit smoking save around £250

each month which is a lot of money, and there are a multitude of worthwhile things you can spend this money on such as a holiday, treating your family, buying new clothes, joining a gym or a fitness class. The options are endless and what better ways to treat yourself and your family, than poison yourself! All you need to do is to work out how much money you spend on cigarettes and you'll see just how much you can save. Not only will you save money from buying cigarettes but you will also save money from smoking related items like ashtrays, lighters, chewing gums, perfumes and other fresh breath and odour products. In addition to this you will save money on health care treatments for smoking related problems, and also overcome problems with gaining affordable life insurance.

4. Longevity

Abstaining from smoking adds years on your lifespan and also greatly improves your chances of a disease-free life in old age. Half of long-term smokers die early from smoke related diseases like lung cancer, heart disease, stroke and chronic bronchitis. Research has consistently shown that smoking reduces life expectancy by seven to eight years.

Common reasons smokers give to quit smoking

- My chances of getting cancer, heart disease, stroke and other diseases will go down
- I will have more money to spend on myself and loved ones

- I will have peace of mind that I am not putting my loved ones' lives at risk
- I will feel less stressed and anxious
- I will be setting a good example to my children
- I will have more energy
- My breath will be fresh
- It will boost my confidence and self-esteem having the courage to quit
- My food will taste better
- My blood pressure will go down
- I will smell better as will my house, clothes, car
- I will cough less
- I will be less likely to catch colds and flu
- My fingers and nails will not be stained anymore
- I will have healthier skin
- My sense of smell will be boosted
- I will have a higher chance of conceiving
- My unborn baby will have a better chance of being born healthy
- I will have a good chance of living longer to see my children and grandchildren grow up

Think of your own reasons for quitting smoking, list them and use them as motivators. Pin this list somewhere you can see it easily or access it like your work table, fridge, cupboard or bedside cabinet and every time you think of smoking, remind yourself of the reasons you choose to quit smoking and why you want to stay smoke free. See below for Table of time-related stop smoking benefits.

Time since quitting	Health benefits of quitting
20 Minutes	Pulse returns to normal
8 Hours-	Nicotine is reduced by 90% Carbon-dioxide levels in blood reduce by 75% Circulation improves
24 Hours-	Carbon-dioxide and nicotine almost eliminated from body Lungs start to clear out smoking debris
48 Hours-	All traces of nicotine are removed from the body. Taste and smell improves
72 Hours-	Breathing is easier Bronchial tubes begin to relax Energy levels increase
2-12 Weeks-	Circulation improves
1 Month-	Physical appearance improves, skin becomes less wrinkled
3-9 Months-	Coughing and wheezing is reduced
1 Year-	Excess risk of heart attack reduces by half
10 years-	Risk of lung cancer falls to about half that of a smoker
15 years-	Risk of heart attack falls to the same level of a non-smoker

Chapter Six

The Stop Smoking Plan

If you are contemplating stopping smoking, make a decision to quit now and get on with it, as excuses and doubts will confuse you and put you off. In the main, people who succeed at quitting smoking are people who make the decision to stop and stick with that decision. It takes will-power!

The stages of change when quitting smoking

Originally developed in the late 1970's and early 1980's by James Prochaska and Carlo Di'clemente, the Stages of Change Model (SCM) views behaviour changes as a dynamic process. This model has been applied to a broad range of behaviours including smoking cessation. According to this model, quitting smoking does not happen in one step, people progress through five stages on the way to successful change. In each stage, a person will wrestle with a range of issues and tasks that relate to their smoking behaviour.

These stages are;

1. Pre-contemplation

In the pre-contemplation stage, the smoker is not really thinking about quitting. People in this stage will spend little time thinking about their smoking and may also not view their habit as a problem. They will tend to defend their smoking habit if other people put pressure on them to quit and therefore won't have any intention of taking any action in the near future, which is defined as six months in this model.

2. Contemplation

In contemplation, the smoker seriously thinks about quitting sometime in the near future (often six months). People in this stage are more aware of the personal consequences of their smoking and they spend a lot of time thinking about their smoking habit as a problem, therefore they are more open to receiving information about smoking and more likely to use educational interventions and reflect on their own feelings, thoughts and behaviours concerning smoking.

3. Preparation

In the preparation stage, people have made the decision to quit and are getting ready to stop smoking. They can now see the positives/pros of smoking as outweighing the negatives/cons. They are less uncertain now about quitting and may also be smoking fewer cigarettes or delaying their first cigarette of the day and also setting a date to quit smoking.

4. Action

In this stage, people are actively involved in taking steps to stop smoking using different methods. People in this stage are making overt efforts to stop smoking and are at the greatest risk of relapse. They will be more open to receiving help and believe they have sufficient autonomy to change their smoking behaviour. They are likely to seek support from others, for instance from family and close friends and will mentally review their commitment to themselves and develop plans to deal with both personal and external pressures that may cause relapses. This stage will generally last up to six months. This is a period during which smokers need the most help and support as they will be more vulnerable to relapsing.

5. Maintenance

This is the last stage that involves being able to successfully avoid any temptations to smoke again. People in this stage are able to anticipate the situation in which a relapse could occur and prepare coping strategies in advance. If they slip and have a cigarette, they will resist regarding themselves as having failed. They will rather view the incidence as an indication that they have to learn to cope differently and analyse how the slip happened. This gives them a stronger sense of self-control and ability to get back on track. They will also tend to remind themselves of how much progress they've made coming this far.

Relapse

Along the way to permanently quitting smoking, most people experience a relapse. A relapse is often accompanied by feelings of discouragement and seeing oneself as a failure.

While a relapse can be discouraging, the majority of people who successfully quit do not follow a straight path, they rather cycle through the five stages of change several times before reaching the stage of quitting for good.

Relapse is a normal occurrence along the way to quitting. It is important for the smoker to look at exactly why they relapsed and make plans to cope if faced with similar circumstances in the future. A relapse can be an important opportunity for learning and becoming stronger or it can be an excuse to give up, especially when a person feels an immediate sense of defeat and failure. The key to recovering from a relapse is to review the quit attempt up to that point. Identify personal strengths and weaknesses, and develop plans to resolve your weaknesses to solve similar problems the next time they occur. People who have relapsed may need to learn to anticipate high risk situations more effectively, control environmental cues that tempt them to smoke like being around friends or family who smoke, and also learn how to handle unexpected episodes of stress without smoking.

Cognitive Dissonance in smoking

Before we explore the stop smoking plan, I will explain a little about Cognitive Dissonance, a theory in psychology which refers to a situation involving conflicting attitudes, beliefs and behaviours. A majority of people, mainly non-smokers, tend to be confused as to why a person would continue to smoke when they understand the risks it carries. Cognitive dissonance suggests that actually many people who smoke know the dangers but will act in ways that contradict their beliefs. They will change their beliefs to align with their behaviours, hence producing a feeling of discomfort leading to an alteration in one of the attitudes, beliefs or behaviours to reduce the discomfort and restore balance.

Many smokers know that smoking puts their lives at risk but they carry on smoking, justifying their actions or behaviour in denial by saying things like "I know of many smokers who lived long lives" or "Its not as bad as they make it out to be". Cognitive dissonance shows that human beings do not want to be proved wrong so they will do whatever it takes to show that they are right even to the point of limiting educative information on smoking and only focusing on what fits into their beliefs, consequently putting their lives in grave danger.

Self-efficacy in quitting smoking

Self-efficacy is a social-cognitive theory by psychologist Albert Bandura. It is defined as one's belief in their ability to succeed in specific situations or accomplish a task, in this case quitting smoking. Successful smoking cessation has been linked to a person's confidence in their ability to quit, in particular abstaining from smoking and feeling less temptation.

People who really believe that they can quit smoking have a greater chance of success than those who don't. Therefore belief is very important in the stop smoking process.

Self-efficacy plays an indispensable role in the way we think, feel and behave. If you think about quitting smoking with a positive mental attitude, you will be able to resist the temptation to smoke again. You will also feel positive which will consequently result in positive healthy behaviours, for example instead of lighting up a cigarette, you will go for a walk or listen to relaxing music. This will have a positive impact on your confidence, as temptation and confidence have strong inverse correlations, for instance as temptation goes down, confidence goes up. The difference between temptation and confidence decreases with progress through the process of quitting smoking. A strong sense of self-efficacy will help in smoking cessation in the following ways. You will be able to;

- Recover quickly from setbacks and disappointments
- Develop deeper interest in the activities and hobbies in which you partake
- View problems or setbacks as tasks to be mastered or lessons to be learned
- Have a stronger sense of commitment to whatever you set your mind on or to personal goals
- Have a more positive mental attitude
- Have a boost in confidence/self-esteem

Will-power in quitting smoking

To quit smoking you need a certain amount of will-power, which we all possess fortunately! But it all comes down to whether you use it or not. People always claim that they don't have enough will power to stop smoking, and what they do is wait around for a miraculous day to come along when they have will power so that they can stop smoking, which is of course wishful thinking as that day will never come along. Quite simply the power lies in stopping today and now.

Motivation in the process of quitting smoking
Motivation is the inner power that pushes us to achieve a goal and is one of the most important keys to success that can be applied to any action or goals, including stopping smoking. Motivation is a key factor to helping smokers give up their health damaging behaviour. Ask yourself why quitting smoking is important to you? And if so what are the reasons? Make those reasons your motivations to quit, you are more likely to succeed if you are doing this for yourself other than doing it to please others. A motivated mind will take you far in your attempt to stop smoking making it easy for you to choose behaviours that will support your new lifestyle. However if you lack motivation then your chances of succeeding will be limited. Common motivators when quitting smoking are;

- Health for both the smoker and family
- To save money
- To have a baby
- Fed up of foul smell in the home, car, clothes
- To take back control

- Sports performance
- For children or partner
- To fit in a non-smoking social circle

If none of these is relevant to you then find something that you are emotionally attached to, use this as your motivator, a place, a person, something or things, the more emotional ties you have with your motivator the better.

To stay motivated

- Set yourself goals and pinpoint them, make the decision to stop and stick with it.
- After you make the decision to stop, be persistent. Whatever the challenges try and look for ways to hang in there not for ways out!
- Don't give up and give in to smoking again.
- Be aware not to keep the company of smokers especially in the early days of your quitting smoking when you are more likely to be tempted. Socialise with non-smokers or other people who are trying to quit as they will keep you motivated.
- The benefits of quitting smoking must outweigh the pleasure you achieve from smoking.
- Be positive- a positive attitude and outlook is very important and will help you quit easier. Get rid of any negative thoughts and any fear of failure, you shouldn't think of failure as an option.

- Enjoy the process and don't feel as though you have been forced to stop smoking, see your decision as one of the best you have made in your life.
- You must want to change more than you want to smoke!

The smoke free plan or diary

Keeping a smoking diary will help you to record your smoking habits and learn what triggers them, for instance when you smoke, why you smoke, where you smoke. And after identifying these patterns you can begin to change your habits by finding new ways to cope or deal with your trigger or triggers.

When

I smoke when I'm feeling: **YES   NO**

Bored
Sad
Lonely
Stressed
To Relax
Socialise

Why   **YES   NO**

I smoke when I need to:

Be loved

Relax

Be comforted

Pass time

Fit in-

Where I smoke   **YES**   **NO**

At work

At social events

Watching television

In the car/driving

At meals

New coping strategies

When   **New Option**

----------------------------   ---------------------

----------------------------   ---------------------

----------------------------   ---------------------

----------------------------   ---------------------

----------------------------   ---------------------

Why   **New Option**

----------------------------   ---------------------

----------------------------   ---------------------

----------------------------   ---------------------

----------------------------   ---------------------

----------------------------   ---------------------

----------------------------   ---------------------

Where	**New Option**
--------------------------	---------------------
--------------------------	---------------------
--------------------------	---------------------

New options should be activities that you are genuinely interested in, since this will make it easier for you to commit to them. These may include going for a walk or any form of exercise, calling a friend/ family, making a cup of tea, writing down your feelings, visiting a friend, gardening, cooking, walking the dog, listening to motivating music, reading, practicing relaxation exercises, deep breathing, yoga, meditation, prayer.

**

Chapter Seven

Smoking and the Mind

The mind is a very powerful tool that holds the key to the way we think, feel and behave. On top of that, our attitudes, beliefs and habits are stored and controlled in the subconscious part of the mind, which means that every learned habit like smoking is stored in the subconscious mind. This is why it is so crucial in any quit smoking interventions to begin making any changes here exerting emphasis on the subconscious mind. This is the main reason why hypnosis is one of the most successful and highly effective therapies in stop smoking. Smoking is a habit and as such, becomes an inherent part of your learned behaviour.

Belief is another important aspect in any quit smoking process, beliefs are assumptions that we hold to be true about ourselves and others. These beliefs may either be positive or negative and are also stored in the subconscious mind, where they are deeply ingrained strongly influencing and guiding our behaviours. If your beliefs are negative and self limiting in nature they will act in a way that proves exactly that. On the other hand positive empowering beliefs will power you on to reach your goals. Previous studies have shown that people who believe that they can stop smoking have a greater chance of success.

Examples of positive empowering beliefs
- I will quit smoking
- I believe I can quit smoking
- I am good enough
- I can make this a success
- I am in control of the process

Examples of negative self-limiting beliefs
- I can't stop smoking
- I am not good enough
- I am not good at anything so why bother
- I am worthless
- I am going to fail at this

The good thing is that beliefs are changeable or replaceable but you will have to firstly identify those negative beliefs that are not working for you and then actively replace them with positive new ones. This is a great way to reprogram your subconscious mind to a more desirable mental state that will support your quit smoking task.

Over and above that, the right attitude will also be of great help for you to stop smoking and stay on the right track. More and more people including doctors and scientists are turning their attention to positive thinking because it is a powerful tool for transforming health and personal development.

Researchers are continuing to find increasing evidence pointing to the numerous benefits of positive thinking, thus it is an important factor in the quit smoking process. Focusing on the positive aspects of stopping smoking will expand your chances of quitting.

Make your thoughts as positive as possible to make the process easier. The mind is so powerful that whatever you consistently think about you will achieve. On that basis the decisions you make as you go along will be heavily based on your thoughts. Positive thinking will also help you weed out all negative thoughts about failure, beliefs and behaviours that can sabotage your quit-smoking process. Sad to say, negative thoughts about smoking sometimes spill over as negative feelings and destructive behaviours.

The brainwashed mind

The term brainwash refers to a change in a person's thoughts, beliefs or attitudes as a result of structured consistent manipulative means to persuade individuals to conform to the brainwasher's wishes.

As we have seen, tobacco manufacturers are very clever and know very well how the subconscious mind operates and the power it can have over your thoughts and actions, so they spend a lot of time coming up with ways to manipulate your behaviour to buy cigarettes. This is done by cleverly selecting images and scenes that will provoke your emotions and behaviour in the direction they desire, and in doing so repeatedly brainwashing you. Tobacco industries spend billions of dollars on advertising, promotion and sponsorship to primarily target and hook both young and old into smoking using large posters, magazine adverts and movies bombarding their targets with messages like 'smoking gives you confidence' 'smoking relaxes you, 'smoking gives you the edge' 'smoking concentrates you' or 'it relieves stress'.

Brainwashers tend to target those who are vulnerable, that is why when you look at the many ways people start smoking in the main they are in vulnerable situations. For example, many people start smoking as teenagers because of peer pressure, being bullied at school or trying to cope with the many changes that are taking place in their bodies and minds. In other cases people smoke when they are stressed, sad, anxious, depressed, desperately trying to lose weight and so forth.

Brainwashing also attacks and impacts the victim's self-confidence by breaking them down either mentally, physically or emotionally. Once the victim is brainwashed into smoking they will get hooked on nicotine, inadvertently spending a lot of their hard earned money on their new smoking habit. This is ultimately the desired intention of the tobacco manufacturers, to extort money from its victims.

Once people are hooked on smoking, they are then brainwashed with messages about how hard and impossible it is to quit the habit. This is another reason why people carry on smoking for a long time, because their subconscious minds have been bombarded repeatedly with these sort of messages, that quitting smoking will be a huge task so they give up before they even try! Which of course isn't true at all, actually giving up smoking is not impossible and no one is destined to a life of smoking if they don't want to. Thousands of people give up smoking everyday so can you. Nicotine withdrawal symptoms do not cause any pain but nonetheless are not to be ignored. The cravings will disappear as time goes by without smoking, the cravings and longings for a smoke are programmed in your subconscious mind but will pass as time goes by. Mind techniques are very effective and powerful in re-programming your mind to change your thoughts, habits, behaviours and attitudes towards smoking. It is easy and achievable, and remember you were a non-smoker before so you can be a non-smoker again if you choose to.

The fearful mind

Fear is one of life's common human emotions and one we must learn to deal with. Many smokers develop profound fear about ending their nicotine use, sometimes this fear is part of the addiction whereas sometimes its baseless. Fear often prevents smokers from reaching out to take action to kick smoking out of their lives, predominantly they will be scared of things like failure or relapsing, pain associated with nicotine withdrawal symptoms, losing smoking friends, gaining weight, losing control, inability to deal with stress, not being able to relax, losing identity, losing enjoyment and life becoming boring or unpleasant, not being able to sleep at night or enjoy their meals again, the list goes on.

Mostly the things that smokers are fearful of have no truth in them and usually replacing these fears with knowledge and awareness is always of great benefit. Giving in to fear is one way of giving up your power because normally whatever you focus on grows thus giving it the power to control you, so don't let this fear put you off before you even start.

Points to consider

- Identify what your fears are about quitting smoking.
- Develop an understanding of what you are afraid of and also educate yourself about those fears.
- Talk about your fears with a professional, sharing your fears will make them less daunting.
- Concentrate more on the end result or the outcome and every successful step you take. This kind of mindset will help alleviate your fears.

Chapter Eight

Stop Smoking Therapies

Hypnotherapy

Research has shown that hypnosis is very effective in beating smoking addiction, more successful than nicotine therapy alone. People are often curious about hypnosis and the first question they always ask is: does hypnosis work and how does it work? Hypnosis is a state of deep relaxation. When you are under hypnosis you stay awake though very deeply relaxed. There have been misconceptions about hypnosis such as that when you are under the influence of hypnosis you are not in control, or you may not wake up and that hypnosis is mind manipulation or that it is a supernatural practice none of which are true. Hypnosis has been used as a therapy since the 18th century, when Franz Anton Mesmer started using it as a therapeutic tool, but in actual fact the history of hypnosis goes further back than Mesmer.

Many ancient cultures including Egyptians, Chinese, Greeks, Persians, Romans, Indians, Hebrews, used hypnosis in some form in places that were formally termed as sleep or dream temples. Hypnosis was used to treat both physical and mental ailments using suggestion therapy to induce a deep trance or sleep. Hypnosis is a safe and healthy way of quitting smoking no chemicals or side effects! Because the subconscious mind stores the root of many problems, hypnosis is a natural, easy and effective technique for accessing the subconscious and re-programming it to accept new positive changes.

Smoking as a habit or addiction starts in the mind and what makes hypnosis a powerful tool is that while under hypnosis your subconscious mind will be open to the positive healthy suggestions it is fed, replacing any old smoking habits, attitudes, beliefs and behaviours with positive new ones which will in return help you to break your smoking chain.

To sum it up, hypnotherapy works so rapidly with bad habits like smoking because it works directly with the subconscious mind by bypassing the critical conscious mind and getting to the root of the problem so that necessary changes can be made. Not only does hypnosis make positive changes within you, it also relaxes you and helps relieve the stress and anxiety of withdrawal symptoms, which is another bonus.

The Hypnotherapy session

The hypnotherapist will first and foremost establish rapport with you the client encouraging you to open up about your concerns. They will also take your medical history, your motivations for quitting, your smoking timetable and establish the factors why you are giving up smoking. They will explore the facts about smoking with you to give you a clear view of the situation you are in or a reality check about smoking and the positive benefits for you giving up smoking. Goals for your therapy will be discussed and agreed and they will also tell you more about what hypnosis is and how it works. A date will be set for your first session, which will usually last one and a half hours followed by subsequent sessions.

There are so many people out there who are not comfortable opening up about their experiences to a therapist. People who want to take the power of their recovery in their own hands, are highly motivated and would rather save money and take the route of self-therapy, if you are one of these individuals then self-hypnosis is for you. However, like other therapies hypnosis is not for everyone, it can work wonders for you and not so much for the next person, also people with serious mental illness like psychosis, personality disorders, or those under the influence of drugs or alcohol are not advised to use hypnosis in any form.

Self-hypnosis script recording

Below are two different styles of self-hypnosis scripts which you can try and test to see which one works for you, If none of these scripts suit your circumstances you should go ahead and add whatever it is you want to add. However, the way you present or deliver your script is equally important, for instance the tone of your voice, the pace at which you pronounce words and the emotion in your voice.

Tone of your voice- your voice should be calm, comfortable and relaxed.

The speed or pace- choose a pace that suits you, slow or slightly fast.

Emotion- the emotion in your voice should be kind, caring, compassionate, confident and understanding. Avoid sounding cold, detached and uncaring. This is very important, as your voice is going to be your guide to encourage you to enter a deep relaxed hypnotic state, also concentrate on the words and images you are creating.

Once you have finished recording your script, go back through it, if it doesn't sound how you like, you may make more attempts, practice makes perfect. There are many people who are uncomfortable with their voices, if you are one of them, find someone to record it for you. You can add some background music if you feel this will work for you, feel free to experiment with different ideas.

Once you are satisfied with your recording, the next thing will be to get started. You will need a calm and quiet spot with no background noises, slot into a comfortable position and listen to your script. Be yourself and go with the flow, don't try and force yourself into hypnosis, it will just happen naturally as you relax deeper and deeper. Practice everyday and do not despair because you haven't seen any results, some people need more attempts before they see changes and for others it just happens fast. We are all different and therefore adapt to hypnosis at different paces. The scripts below can be altered to suit the user. Script one is in the first person therefore ready to use directly to yourself with no need for someone to read it to you, whereas the second script can be read out to you. However, if you prefer not to involve another person you can still alter it, record it and get going.

Quit Smoking Script 1

I will close my eyes and move myself into the most comfortable position I can......throughout this whole experience I will be in total control ...... I will always be aware .....the state that I will achieve is a completely natural state that will assist me to make the changes that I have sensibly decided to make from today and onwards ......I will start by concentrating on my breathing ...... and as I do so the outside noises will begin to become irrelevant ...... and as I use the powerful ability of my subconscious mind to concentrate on my breathing ...... helping me to achieve the positive beneficial state for accomplishing my goal of quitting smoking ......

Now I move on to relaxing my body ...... all my muscles from top to bottom ...... I begin with the muscles in my face by relaxing, relaxing, relaxing them ......The muscles of my neck are slowly loosening and relaxing, relaxing, relaxing ...... The muscles of my shoulders are loosening their stiffness and are relaxing, relaxing .... Both my hands are totally free and their muscles are relaxing, relaxing, relaxing .... The muscles in my stomach are relaxing and loosening up, I am floating deeper and deeper into a soothing relaxation ....

And now I am feeling the muscles in my legs and toes relax, my entire body feels very comfortable ...... just drifting and floating ...... deeper, deeper relaxed ......

As I am relaxing deeper and deeper ...... I begin to imagine a peaceful and special place for me ..... I can see it ...... feel it ...... I am alone and there is no one to interrupt me ..... I can feel a sense of positive feelings in this peaceful place ...... growing stronger and stronger .... and relaxing deeper and deeper....... the stresses and tensions are bouncing off away from me ...... bouncing away ....from me. And these positive feelings will stay with me and grow stronger and stronger throughout the day .....tomorrow and the days after ......

Now that I'm in my special place and deeply relaxed I reflect for a moment on all the things I have achieved in the past ...... the goals I have reached and all of the positive things in my life ...... I feel proud of myself and have no doubt that I will continue to achieve more goals in every area of my life ..... I'm more determined than ever before to reject my habit of smoking cigarettes ...... I have all the right reasons to be a non-smoker ...... for my health ..... my family ..... and my finances ..... my mind rejects smoking so does my body I

Imagine myself throwing a packet of cigarettes out of the window away from me and that feels fine .

I'm a non-smoker and that feels fine ...... my lungs no longer want those poisonous fumes in them ..... they will now become clean .... clear and healthy once again ...... the smell of cigarettes is now disgusting ...... and the taste is unappealing and unappetising ......my mouth is clear of smoke .... without any trace of cigarette taste and it feels fresh ...... my taste buds experience the appetising fresh tastes of food ...... and that feels wonderful ....

There are no poisonous fumes in my system any more ...... I choose to be healthy ...... to breath clean air ...... my lungs are clean and healthy ...... I am a non-smoker and have made up my mind ...... and I am now more motivated than ever to continue to create the most healthy and positive life for myself ...... and I am now a non-smoker ...... I feel it within .... I now make a conscious choice not to smoke ...... and emotionally I feel fine..... I am a non-smoker and will remain a non- smoker ...... I see myself doing my daily routines without a cigarette .....and feeling just fine ..... being a non-smoker suits me well. I now have new ways of dealing with my old habits .....such as at work I will have to go for a walk at break time ..... make a cup of tea ..... snack on fruit ....or join my non-smoking work mates .....and at social events I will join the non-smokers ...... go out with non-smoking friends ..... and at home I will keep myself busy ...... I will go for a run ...... read a

book I like ...... go for a walk ...... or make a cup of tea ......
these are my new ways of dealing with my old habits ...... this
is a successful way ..... it works and I feel fine .... I imagine
my daily routine without a cigarette .....calm and relaxed .....
there is a smile on my face ...... and I feel just fine .... it feels
wonderful ..... and because I am a non-smoker I begin to
notice that every aspect of my life begins to improve more
and more ...... every day and night ...... I breath more easily
and have new found energy ...... I am a non-smoker ..... I enjoy
being a non-smoker .... I enjoy the benefits of being a non-
smoker...... It feels great without a cigarette .... I AM A NON-
SMOKER.

I will continue to enjoy my special place for a few more
minutes .... enjoy the positive feelings ...... and continue
relaxing .... floating higher and higher into a deep relaxation
.... and I will count from one to five ...... and when I count to
five I will open my eyes and come back to full awareness
feeling calm .... peaceful ...... and relaxed .....

One .... Slowly, calmly and easily returning to awareness
Two ....Each muscle in my body is feeling loose and relaxed
Three ....Feeling perfect in every way
Four .... Beginning to open my eyes
Five .... I open my eyes and come back feeling rejuvenated
             and relaxed

**

Quit smoking script 2

Now just make yourself as comfortable as you can ...... you may like to move around a little until you feel that you are as comfortable as you can possibly be .....start by concentrating on your breathing ...... focussing on each breathe in and each breathe out ..... noticing how your breathing becomes deeper and deeper .... Feel the breathe going through your body starting the process of relaxation ...... you may like to close your eyes now to enjoy the experience more deeply .... Or you may let them close when they are ready ...... when they no longer wish to stay open ...... whatever feels right for you is fine .....

As you concentrate on your breathing you may start to notice that all the everyday noises around you will become irrelevant to you .....helping you to relax even deeper and deeper..... This feeling of relaxation starts at the top of your head ...... soothing and relaxing all those muscles in your scalp ...... feel them relaxing and letting go ...... this feeling carries on now flowing down to your face .....into all those muscles around your eyes ..... cheeks and jaw ...... you feel them dropping and relaxing completely .....

This feeling travels on to your neck ...... as you let this wonderful feeling flow through you ....you find yourself relaxing even deeper and deeper ...... letting go of all the tension in this area .....the relaxation touching every fibre and cell in your body ....

This relaxation feeling travels on now gently into your shoulders ...... soothing them as you release them ...... this wave of relaxation travels on through your arms and fingers ......

The relaxation now travels through your chest .... You notice that your breathing is now deeper .....relaxing you even more and more ...... your body is experiencing how lovely this feels ...... the relaxation flows down into your stomach muscles ..... soothing and calming its way through to your hips ...... travelling further down to your legs ..... thighs and letting them smooth out ......

This feeling travels on to your knees and calves relaxing them completely ...... and then to your feet and toes ...... feeling you with deep and total relaxation than you have ever felt before .....you are now feeling completely relaxed ...... your mind and body becoming one and at peace ...... as you experience this tranquillity ..... just let your mind drift ..... relax and drift and let your powerful subconscious mind take you wherever it wishes to take you ..... it is ready to be explored ..... and it is easy now because you are completely relaxed ...... this deep relaxation will allow you to explore the depths of your smoking habit .....

You are ready to allow your subconscious mind to make the changes within you so that you can revert from being a smoker to being a non-smoker ....

Now that you have decided to quit smoking ...... this is your own decision that no one has forced you into ...... as you continue to relax in this state ..... let all those negative thoughts come and go ...... feel comfortable and completely relaxed ..... Today is an important day for you .....the day that you have chosen to stop smoking ...... to take back control and be in charge of your thoughts and behaviours towards your smoking habit ...... and because you are now in full control and you've taken the first step to stop smoking ...... to become a non- smoker ...... from now and onwards you will think of yourself as a non-smoker ...... you will feel much better and healthier than you've ever felt before ..... you are happier and you will find that each day you have more energy and breathe more easily too ...... and this feels amazing...... You are strong in your ability not to smoke .....even when you're around smokers you do not feel any desire to join in ..... in fact you can't stand the smell of cigarettes anymore ..... and you feel proud that you did yourself a massive favour to stop smoking ...... smoking doesn't appeal to you anymore ..... you are happy with the freedom you now enjoy without being controlled by your old habit ..... you are in total control now .....Your confidence is high because you've realised that you have more power than ever before to take charge ...... you choose to think smoke free positive thoughts and engage in only healthy behaviours ...... you have overcome your bad habit of smoking ...... and all the negative thoughts behind it ...... you have reached your goal of becoming a non-smoker .....

You feel confident that you are going to stick to your new healthier habits .....and that you will make an effort to, and give 100% to stay a non-smoker and never smoke again ..... you are a non-smoker and you will continue to be a non-smoker for as long as you live ..... this is a commitment for life which you will no doubt succeed at ......

Because you are a non-smoker now ...... you're finding that your health has improved immensely ...... this is because your body is toxic free ...... you nourish it by drinking plenty of water ...... eating healthy food and exercising regularly ...... these are one of your new positive habits ..... which will help you in every part of your life ..... you have overcome your old negative habit and replaced it with positive healthy ones ..... which will sustain you to stay smoke free ..... and that makes you feel accomplished ..... and you find that you now have more and more energy ..... that you continue to put to good use by exercising regularly ...... You feel more relaxed and stress free as result ..... you have done it ..... you have managed to quit smoking ...... you are pleased with yourself ..... with a strong sense of pride and satisfaction ...... You are a non-smoker .... And you will stay a non-smoker ......

Enjoy this relaxation for as long as you wish ...... when you are ready to come back to full awareness ...... I will count from one to five ...... and when I count five you will open your eyes and return to awareness feeling calm and relaxed ......

One ...... Beginning to slowly come back

Two ...... You are coming back to full awareness

Three ..... Feeling calm and relaxed

Four ...... Beginning to open your eyes

Five ...... You open your eyes and come back feeling calm and
relaxed

Cognitive Behavioural Therapy for quitting smoking

Cognitive behavioural therapy or CBT is a psychotherapy used to treat numerous psychological problems from depression, anxiety, panic attacks to fatigue and pain as well as helping people overcome addiction and substance abuse.

CBT is based on changing faulty thought patterns and negative behaviour associated with them.

Thoughts ------------ Feelings ------------ Behaviours

Therefore with CBT, changing the thought patterns combined with new healthy behaviours will effectively help in quitting smoking and also to prevent relapse. Your CBT therapist will help you identify distorted and negative thought patterns, and they will put the emphasis on lessening the fear, hopelessness and doubts that may be warding off any quit smoking interventions.

For some, CBT may not be as effective on its own so may be used in conjunction with other approaches.

Examples of distorted thoughts;

Thoughts	Feelings	Behaviour
I will always be a smoker	Stressed	Carry on smoking
I can't stop smoking	Scared	Postpone stop smoking
I'm addicted, what's the point	Anxious	Less motivated
I won't manage without cigarettes	Sad	More excuses

Changing smoking thinking patterns

The way you think will have a big impact on the way you feel and behave. If you are constantly thinking about your next cigarette, you will immediately feel the urge to smoke which will lead you to lighting up that cigarette and smoking. The behaviour here is the smoking and any action that encourages the smoking. This is why CBT is focussed on changing thinking patterns. When you change the way you think about smoking, the way you feel about smoking will also change, impacting on your behaviours positively.

CBT technique for stop smoking

- Individualised problem solving strategies; These are strategies designed to help deal with challenging situations and environment in the quit smoking process.

- Changing thought patterns; This technique is designed to help with coping better emotionally especially with withdrawal symptoms like stress and anxiety. Other than reach for a cigarette to cope you will go for a walk or have a cup of tea hence diverting the thoughts of "I need a smoke" to " I will go for a walk", "I will have a cup of tea".

- Educate yourself about the quit smoking process; The more information you are equipped with the better as this will help you understand the withdrawal symptoms you may encounter and how to manage them effectively.

- Identifying motivations; These are things or people that are engineering your quitting process for example your children, family, partner, health, longevity, finances, career, places. Your motivators will keep you going.

- Aversion Therapy; Aversion therapy involves associating undesirable behaviour with a behaviour, in this case smoking. Its all about getting you to dislike cigarettes and see them as disgusting, try and list as many negative experiences associated with smoking and why you shouldn't smoke. Think about the times you've stood out in the cold or rain to smoke, the undesirable coughing fits, the countless smoking related arguments you've had with your non-smoker other half and all the cleaning you have had to do to get rid of the cigarette odour.

- Identifying social or environmental cues; Figure out which situations make you smoke, identify them and avoid them. It might be that every time you visit a certain friend you smoke a lot so you will have to cut off visiting this friend because you will never be able to quit smoking with them around.

- Social support; If you are lucky enough to have family and friends who are able to support you in your quitting operation, the better. More so, socialising with non-smoking friends or those who are supportive of you will be of great help. You also have to let your family members know that you are quitting so that they do not smoke around you thereby tempting you back into smoking. You should avoid anyone who tries to set you back or sabotage your efforts to quit. Unfortunately there will always be people who will attempt to set you up for failure!

- Weight gain; As mentioned earlier many people are put off stopping smoking because they are scared of gaining weight. The good news is that CBT can include behavioural training to prevent weight gain by focussing on eating healthy and exercising.

If you are considering having CBT, ask your doctor if they can suggest a local therapist or alternatively, the British Association For Behavioural and Cognitive Therapists (BABCP) keeps a register of all accredited therapists and the British Psychological Society (BPS) has a directory of psychologists who specialise in CBT.

Counselling: The Motivational Interview
Many people feel that they can't quit on their own, and therefore need to talk to someone for support. Among the

most common styles of counselling currently in use in the UK for people who want to quit smoking is the motivational interview, originally designed to help individuals with alcohol abuse but now commonly used with smokers.

Motivational interviewing is a patient-centred counselling technique where the client has one or more sessions. In these sessions they are encouraged by their counsellor to explore and resolve their feelings about quitting smoking. The counsellor follows a non-confrontational non- judgemental style and tries to guide the client towards making a sensible decision. In the five principles of motivational interviewing the counsellor will;

- Express and show empathy towards clients when discussing behaviours, feelings, thoughts and life events. This will build trust and a rapport which will help the client to open up and share more with the counsellor.
- Support and develop discrepancy- to help the clients see and feel how their smoking behaviour threatens important personal goals.
- Deal with resistance - for example when the client seems to be resisting changing their behaviour. In a non-confrontational way, the counsellor gets the client to see and examine different view points hence allowing them to make decisions that they will be able to stick to.
- Support self-efficacy by emphasising a belief in the clients that they are capable of becoming non-smokers and can

achieve their goal just as they have achieved other goals in their lives.

- Autonomy- counsellors demonstrate to clients that the power to quit smoking will come from within them not from the counsellor or anyone else. This instils in the client that they are responsible for changing their behaviour.

Motivational interviewing recognises and accepts that clients who need to make changes in their lives approach counselling at different levels of readiness to change their behaviour. During counselling some clients may not yet have taken steps to make those changes themselves, whereas other clients may be actively trying to change their behaviour. The therapist will be actively aiming at succeeding at motivational interviewing using four basic interaction skills which are:

-Using open ended questions;
-Providing affirmations;
-Reflectively listening to the client
-Providing summary statements.

Motivational interventions are both for clients who are not willing to make an attempt to quit their smoking behaviour and those who express interest in quitting. These can be divided into 5 basic types which are:
-Relevance
-Risks
-Rewards

-Roadblocks

-Repetition

Also known as the 5Rs these are helpful when the therapist asks the client a set of questions in relation to their smoking. Hearing their own answers helps the clients to strengthen their motivation and commitment to becoming non-smokers.

1. Relevance: The individual's personal reasons for quitting. The counsellor will ask the client why quitting is personally relevant to them.
2. Risks: Understanding the short and long-term risks of smoking. The counsellor will ask the client to identify potential pitfalls of smoking and also highlight and suggest the ones that are more relevant to the client.
3. Rewards: Identifying the benefits of stop smoking. The therapist will ask the client to identify the benefits of quitting smoking especially the ones they relate with.
4. Roadblocks: Acknowledging the barriers to quitting smoking. The counsellor will ask you to identify barriers or blocks to your quitting.
5. Repetition: Going over these points at each session. You will repeat the motivational intervention every time you see your therapist or counsellor.

Positive Thinking and Affirmations in quit smoking

Positive thinking has become very popular in recent times as more and more people awaken to the fact that they can change their circumstances by adjusting their way of thinking. People who are optimistic are better at dealing with problems because they view these problems as temporary setbacks and therefore will try as much as they can to positively move through the challenges they are presented with without denying reality. This same attitude is required in the quit smoking process. For success to be attained, you have to adapt a positive mental attitude owing to the fact that we all have the power and prerogative to choose our thoughts, therefore always strive to make yours positive.

You have to think positively and expect good and favourable outcomes, focussing on your thoughts, visions and actions that are conducive to productivity and quit smoking success. Truth is you will never be successful if you expect to fail. With a negative attitude you will always expect the worst outcomes because you will view your smoking as a long-term problem that will never go away. This is a self limiting, unhealthy way of thinking. Affirmations are simple but powerful statements aimed at affecting and helping the subconscious mind to make positive changes.

Affirmations can help develop a powerful attitude to quit smoking because the subconscious mind accepts every command or suggestion given to it. It is therefore a great way to create positive thoughts, attitudes, habits, beliefs and behaviours. If used continuously, affirmations will eventually breakdown even the strongest resistance. Repeating affirmations will help you to overcome negative thoughts or feelings about smoking and yourself, thence assisting you to change and help establish a permanent change in your belief system. You can add to the affirmations below or make up your own, based on your needs and circumstances as there is no one fit for all.

Helpful quit smoking affirmations

- Smoking is not part of me anymore
- Smoking doesn't define me
- I choose healthy behaviours
- I am willing to change my habits
- I choose to live a smoke free life
- I successfully quit smoking
- I am positive about my choices
- I choose life over bad health
- The thought of smoking appals me
- I find the smell of cigarettes nauseating
- I love and enjoy the smoke free fresh air
- My food tastes better
- My vision is better
- My skin is glowing
- My breath is fresh
- I am in the best health of my life
- Smoking is in my past and I detest it
- Life is much better as a non-smoker
- I engage in behaviours that nourish my well-being
- Eliminating nicotine and cravings in my life is effortless

- I am able to release old habits
- I am worthy of a healthy smoke free life
- I am stronger than any habit or addiction
- I am finally in control of my life
- I am a non-smoker

**

Deep Breathing Technique in stop smoking

Breathing awareness and good breathing habits will promote your psychological and physical well-being. Whether done on its own or combining it with the relaxation technique, this technique can prove beneficial to health. When you breath in you obtain oxygen and release carbon-dioxide which is a waste product. Poor breathing reduces the flow of oxygen into the body and carbon-dioxide out of the body. Practicing the deep breathing technique calms your mind and relaxes your body too, inevitably also balancing oxygen and carbon-dioxide levels in your body. Deep breathing is an invaluable tool in stopping smoking that will help you with relieving nicotine withdrawal symptoms and stress.

During the quit smoking process, breathing exercises can also be done to replace the desire for a puff. Another bonus is that breathing technique can be practiced safely by almost everyone and everywhere. For those who are looking for more natural ways to quit smoking, this is one of the methods that will help you alongside relaxation technique, CBT,

Counselling, hypnotherapy, NLP(Neuro-Linguistic Programming) and acupuncture.

Breathing Exercise

- Choose a time and place to practice without being disturbed or interrupted .....
- Make sure you maintain a good posture and you don't fall asleep .....
- Breath in through your nose let the breathe flow deeply down into your abdomen comfortably. Breath in though your nose and out through your mouth .....
- You should feel more and more relaxed as you continue to breath in and out .....
- Practice breathing in and out for as long as you want to
- When you have mastered the technique, start applying it to quitting smoking, for instance when you are experiencing urges to smoke, withdrawal symptoms, stressful situations, both smoke related and non-smoke related. The breathing exercise will relieve tension and anxiety from your mind and body.

Progressive Muscle Relaxation(PMR)

Many people smoke to relieve the stressful situations they are facing. Even when presented with the risks associated with smoking, some smokers will continue smoking and find it hard to stop in order to combat their stress. However, smoking doesn't take away the problems that cause the stress. The best way to deal with stress is confronting the root cause of the problem other than treating smoking as your long time reliever. You should also find more healthier and effective ways to relieve stress like the PMR, deep breathing technique, meditation, self-hypnosis, yoga, exercise and many more. The PMR can also be very helpful in dealing with withdrawal symptoms in the process of quitting smoking in a way that it relaxes you, lowering your tension and stress levels.

Progressive Muscle Relaxation technique

- Find a quiet place
- Sit comfortably with a straight back with both feet on the floor, rest your arms on your lap .....
- Breath in through your nose into your abdomen slowly and relax ......
- Close your eyes and direct your attention to your face, around your eyes, concentrate on the muscles here, tense them, feel their tightness and then relax them ...... letting all the tenseness fade away .....
- Now move to your jaw and neck, there is always a lot of tension in this area ...... hold for five seconds and then relax these muscles .... feel them loosen up and relax ......
- Move on to the muscles in your shoulders ...... tense them and release ...... feel them relax .....
- Bring your focus to your hands .....tense the muscles in your hands and hold ..... concentrate on the tenseness, drop them and let them relax ......

- Now move on further to your chest and stomach muscles, tense and tighten them ...... hold for 5 seconds and relax them .....
- Breath in and fill your lungs ...... then breath out deeply through your abdomen and direct your attention to your back ..... tense it ..... and relax ..... letting all the tension dissolve away .....
- Tighten your thigh and buttock muscles ....relax them and feel the difference ..... now tense your legs and curl your toes experiencing the tension ..... release and relax .....
- As you continue on, you will feel a deep relaxation sweeping through your entire body ....continue to breath in and out gently and deeply ...... relaxing even more and letting go of any residue of aches and pains in your body ...... feeling your whole body completely calm and relaxed.

Acupuncture in the quit smoking process

Acupuncture has proved to be effective in helping people to overcome their tobacco addiction and also dealing with withdrawal symptoms. For this reason acupuncture has seen a rise in drug detox clinics around the world. Acupuncture is based on traditional Chinese medicine. It involves sticking tiny needles into strategic pressure points in the body and leaving them for up to 30 minutes. There are many people who have managed to quit smoking by using acupuncture solely and also others who haven't managed successfully with it. Quitting smoking is a journey of exploring until you find a method that works for you. If you choose to have acupuncture make sure your practitioner is a regulated health care professional or a recognised member of a National Acupuncture Organisation. When carried out by an experienced practitioner, acupuncture is a generally safe therapy.

**

Chapter Nine

Nicotine Replacement Therapy (NRT)

Because cigarettes contain nicotine, when you smoke over a long period of time your body becomes dependent on the nicotine. This is why when you try to stop smoking you will have nicotine withdrawal symptoms. Nicotine Replacement Therapy also known as NRT is a medically approved way of taking nicotine into the blood stream without smoking. It is prescribed by doctors or pharmacists to help people stop smoking. Many people find nicotine cravings extremely difficult to handle when quitting, this is where NRT is useful. NRT will help you manage these withdrawal symptoms, giving you a greater chance of quitting successfully.

The products used are usually nicotine gums, patches, inhalers, tablets, lozenges and sprays and a full course of treatment usually lasts for 8-12 weeks depending on the type you are using. Now, many people may be thinking that why swap one addiction for another, as in cigarettes for NRT. The reality is that NRT is safer than smoking as smoking is highly addictive because it delivers nicotine at a faster rate to the brain making stopping very difficult, whereas the nicotine level in NRT is much lower than tobacco. The way NRT delivers nicotine in the body makes it less addictive than the nicotine in tobacco.

In spite of that, it is safer to use licensed nicotine products instead of smoking tobacco, most of the damage in smoking is caused by components in tobacco other than nicotine. NRT is suitable for most adults but for people who suffer from heart or circulatory conditions, breast feeding mothers or who are pregnant, check with your doctor.

Nicotine also affects blood sugar levels, so people with diabetes on NRT should regularly check their blood sugar levels. Nevertheless, if you are thinking of using NRT it is best that you take time to investigate each of the different options and work out which will suit you best, and if one doesn't work for you, you can always try another one, as there are so many options to choose from.

It is also important to note that Nicotine Replacement Therapies do not come without side effects for example skin irritation from patches, irritation of the nose, throat or eyes from nasal sprays, disturbed sleep, upset stomach, dizziness and headaches among others.

To clarify, nicotine products will not stop you from smoking, they will reduce your urges to smoke and the unpleasant feelings caused by withdrawal symptoms. Although many people find that using two NRT's at the same time makes a big difference in relieving cravings and withdrawal symptoms.

The Nicotine Patch

This is one of the many NRT's proven to help people ease nicotine withdrawal symptoms. You wear this patch on the skin where it slowly releases nicotine which is absorbed into your body though your skin. These can reduce or even stop withdrawal symptoms associated with smoking cessation if the dosage and duration is rightly followed correctly.

Side effects

- Redness, skin irritation and itching where the patch is stuck
- Changes in sleeping patterns and discomfort while wearing the patch during the night
- Headaches
- Nausea
- Rapid heartbeat

Nicotine Chewing Gum

This is the most popular NRT being used by about a million smokers in Britain each year. Nicotine gum is a sugar free gum in which nicotine has been attached, so that when you chew it, it slowly releases nicotine in the body through absorption by the tissues of the mouth. Scientific studies have shown that just like other NRT's the nicotine chewing gum increases your chances of successfully quitting smoking.

Side effects

- Sleep disturbances may occur
- Headaches
- Mouth irritation
- Heartburn
- Hiccups in the early days
- Increased heart rate
- Oral irritation
- Dental pain
- Heartburn
- Hiccups

Nicotine Nasal Spray

The nicotine nasal spray can be used to relieve cravings and withdrawal symptoms, you spray once in each nostril up to two times in an hour. It may be particularly helpful to the most heavily dependent smokers because the nicotine is quickly absorbed though the blood vessels in the nose to relieve cravings quickly.

Side effects

- Stinging
- Throat and nasal irritation
- Watering eyes
- Sneezing
- Coughing
- Heartburn
- Headaches

- Shortness of breath
- Dizziness
- Nosebleeds
- Nausea

Inhaler

This looks more like a cigarette made up of a cartridge containing nicotine. When you inhale on it or puff, nicotine vapour comes out of it which is then absorbed through the lining of the mouth and upper oesophagus. The absorption of nicotine with an inhaler is slower than when you are smoking a cigarette. Inhalers tackle the habit of smoking as well as the physical addiction to nicotine. When you puff on the inhaler mouthpiece, the cartridge releases nicotine to help release your craving. Another bonus of the inhaler is that because it is designed as a cigarette your hands are kept busy too.

Side effects

- Stomach upset
- Dizziness
- Vomiting
- Mouth ulcer
- Nasal congestion
- Hiccups
- Sinusitis
- Tearing of eyes
- Runny nose
- Irregular heartbeat

Nicotine Mouth Spray

Nicotine mouth spray is a non-prescription NRT product, which means that you can buy it over the counter. It is designed for the nicotine to be absorbed though the lining of the mouth and it's best not to swallow for a few seconds after spraying. It works the same way as the gum. Research has shown that mouth sprays allow for faster absorption of nicotine compared to nicotine gum or lozenges so may reduce cravings much faster.

Side effects

- Nausea
- Nose tingling or burning
- Mouth dryness
- Indigestion
- Hiccups
- Headaches

Nicotine Lozenges

You suck on nicotine lozenges as you would on a sweet, they dissolve in the mouth to release a dose of nicotine. There are different types with different sizes, amounts of nicotine and flavours, you have to find which one suits you best. Lozenges deliver nicotine into the blood stream at a fast rate.

Side effects

- Insomnia
- Dizziness

- Headaches
- Nausea and vomiting
- Heart palpitations
- Hiccups
- Heartburn

**

Chapter Ten

Stop-Smoking Medicines

Stop-smoking medications can double your chances of quitting smoking. This is due to the fact that they decrease your nicotine cravings and withdrawal symptoms. However stop-smoking drugs have raised concerns due to the fact that like most medications, they carry side effects. Currently there are two main medications prescribed to help people stop smoking on the NHS, which are Zyban (or Bupropion) and Champix also known as Varenicline.

1. Zyban (Buplopion)

Zyban is a medication that was originally designed to treat depression. This particular drug is currently being extensively researched but nevertheless is widely used in many countries around the world. It is believed that this drug works by affecting parts of the brain involved in addictive behaviour. Zyban does not contain nicotine and does not help you to quit smoking the same way NRT does, however it reduces cravings and withdrawal symptoms. To obtain this drug, you have to go to your doctor for a prescription. Zyban is taken 7-14 days before you try to quit, a course of treatment usually lasts 7-9 weeks. Zyban is not suitable for;

-Pregnant or breastfeeding women.

-People with Central Nervous (CNS) Tumours.

-People who suffer from anorexia or bulimia.

-People with severe cirrhosis of liver.

-Those who suffer from epilepsy.

-People with bipolar disorder.

-People with serious alcohol misuse problems.

-Those who are treating diabetes with hypoglycaemia
 medication or insulin.

Side effects of Zyban

- Problems sleeping

- Dizziness

- Drowsiness

- Dry mouth

- Upset stomach

- Stomach pain

- Headaches

- Difficulty concentrating

- Changes in appetite- weight loss or gain

- Loss of interest in intimacy

- Sore throat

- Ringing in the ears

- Increased sweating

2. Champix (Varenicline)

Champix works by preventing nicotine from binding to
receptors (parts of the brain that respond to nicotine) which

reduces the rewarding and reinforcing effects of smoking. It also stimulates nicotine receptors like nicotine does, hence reducing the bad mood swings, agitation and irritation which people may experience when trying to quit smoking. Champix is taken a week before you stop smoking, which gives it a chance to build up in your body so that by the time your body starts to feel withdrawal symptoms, the drug has already taken effect. Champix is recommended to be taken for 12 weeks. However it is not suitable for;

- Children and young people under the age of 18
- Pregnant and breastfeeding women
- Sufferers some mental illnesses
- Those with advanced kidney disease

Side effects
- Nausea and vomiting
- Headaches
- Sleeping difficulties
- Increased appetite
- Dry mouth
- Tiredness, low energy levels
- Dizziness
- Diarrhoea or constipation
- Swollen stomach
- Slow digestion

**

Chapter Eleven

A Review of Lifestyle When Quitting Smoking

Quitting smoking will require you to make changes in your lifestyle. For instance you will have to look at your diet, your exercise levels, your mental attitude, your sleeping pattern, the company you keep and so forth. Consequently, this will allow you to replace your negative behaviours with more positive and healthy ones which will swiftly facilitate the process of quitting smoking.

1. A healthy diet

Maintaining a healthy diet is important throughout the process of stopping smoking and after. Limit sugar, salt and fat intake especially saturated fats, and use more of the mono-unsaturated fats which are found in olive oil or fats from oily fish. Studies have shown that eating fish more than twice a week might help limit tobacco damage in people who do not smoke more than a pack and a half a day. It is very common for people who are quitting smoking to fill their cravings with eating partly because eating gives them something to put in their mouth instead of a cigarette. Those who smoke for comfort or to curb their emotions will tend to replace food as their source of comfort with tobacco. This is why a number of people who are giving up smoking find themselves putting on weight which results in them being put off quitting smoking.

When you quit smoking your taste buds get better and therefore your cravings for nicotine will be more likely to be transferred to food. Be aware of what you snack on throughout the day. This is why it's better to eat a healthy balanced diet which will help you quit and stay healthy. At all costs avoid binge eating, skipping meals and make sure you eat the right portions of food. If you are someone who snacks a lot in between meals, choose only healthy snacks like nuts, seeds, grapes, berries, carrots, cucumber, celery and other healthy bites.

To add to this, drink plenty of water throughout the day to flush out the toxins that nicotine has left in your body, water will also help fill you up so you don't have to snack often. Resist alcohol and caffeine until you are over your cravings, otherwise if you carry on consuming them, they may cause cravings for cigarettes.

NOTE: If you are over-weight or obese and you want to quit smoking but you are worried that you will put on even more weight after quitting smoking, it's best that you stop smoking first and then tackle losing weight after.

**

2. Exercise

Besides preventing weight gain, exercising regularly will play an important part in helping you to quit smoking, more so when you incur a relapse. Keep active as much as you can because this is the time when you need to exercise even more, don't stop or reduce it. Research shows that smokers who follow a regular exercise plan have a much higher success in quitting than those who don't. Smokers often complain of shortness of breath when they are exercising, this is because their lungs have been compromised by smoking. However, after you quit you will slowly start to notice that it becomes easier to exercise as your lung function gets better as it recovers from the effects of inhaling smoke. Even the smallest work-out will help you get back into the routine and also distract you from smoking, as well as:

- Diminishing your stress levels associated with withdrawal symptoms
- Distracting your thoughts of cravings for cigarettes
- Reducing appetite
- Aiding with weight loss and keeping fit
- Fuelling your body with energy

Exercise options

Walking

Skipping

Skating

Swimming

Cycling

Running

Gardening

Aerobics

Hiking

Lifting weights

Team sports

Trampolining

Yoga

Pilates

Boxing

Your exercise will have to be tailored to your needs, for instance what you enjoy doing and what's convenient for you. If you have any disability or illness you can still exercise, generally lighter exercises done in short intervals will benefit you too. For those who are not keen on outside activities or going to the gym, you can try activities in the comfort of your home such as fitness dvd's and websites, youtube, podcasts or on consoles like wii sports.

3. Go to bed early

For most people evenings are the most difficult times of the day in the quit smoking process as there are more temptations to smoke during this time. Therefore it's best to go to bed early everyday to minimise these risks until you are over your cravings.

4.- Change your daily routine

Have a look at situations when you normally smoke and avoid those routines which trigger your smoking, for example if you are in between breaks at work, try and go for a walk instead or have a cup of tea or anything that will break your daily smoking routine.

5. Avoid smokers

Avoid smokers, at least until you are strong enough to be able to do so without being tempted to light up a cigarette. A majority of smokers slip up because someone else is lighting up, moreover many successful ex smokers say that they avoid risking smoking again by avoiding people they know who are smokers.

6. Remove all reminders of smoking

There are many things that will remind you of your smoking which may act as triggers for you to start smoking again. Getting rid of all these reminders will be an important step in quitting smoking. You will have to;

- Get rid of all cigarettes, ashtrays and lighters after your last cigarette.
- Get rid of all the smell of smoke and other reminders of smoking by cleaning your house, clothes, curtains, carpets, upholstery and walls.
- If you smoke in the your car clean it and get rid of lighters, cigarettes and ashtrays.
- Ban people from smoking in your home and car.

Chapter Twelve

Staying On Track

Quitting smoking is a difficult task that will require your effort, time, dedication and will power. In fact a strong desire to smoke can happen weeks, months or years after you've quit. It should be noted that relapses often happen as a result of triggers.

Common relapse triggers to look out for are;

- Stress
- Being in the company of smokers
- Negative attitudes
- Drinking alcohol
- Anxiety
- Poor sleep
- Low energy or tiredness
- Weight gain
- Heavy workload
- Lack of support from friends and family
- Low self-esteem/confidence
- Drinking coffee
- Meals

- Breaks
- Watching television
- Driving

First and foremost to avoid a relapse you have to understand your triggers, these may be places, people, things, or events. Triggers are the causes for your smoking in the first place and can affect you regardless of how long it's been since you stopped smoking.

While many say that smoking helps them to relax, the truth is that nicotine is a stimulant! Relaxation techniques, exercise and deep breathing can all be effective in relieving stress. When you learn to combat stress, you can deal with quitting smoking more easily. If your trigger is your anxiety about your weight gain prior to stopping smoking, concentrate on stopping smoking first and then your weight loss afterwards. Additionally;

- Be positive and stay positive as optimism will help you get through the daily challenges that you will encounter in the process of quitting.
- Negative attitudes should be avoided at all costs as being negative will dampen your moods and also sabotage your efforts. Positive self-talk like " I can do this", " I can quit smoking", " I am capable of succeeding" will also boost your chances. That voice

inside your head has a massive impact on the decisions you make and how you live your life.

- Getting support from your loved ones can play a big role in stopping smoking. Those giving support will help you stay smoke free if you let them know your needs and what they can do to support you. If they are smokers themselves then ask them not to smoke around you and to say no when you ask them for a cigarette.

- Develop a set of strategies that will support your attempts to prevent your old behaviours, habits or beliefs creeping back in and learn how to maintain the new behaviours long enough for them to be reprogrammed into your subconscious mind thus becoming part of your daily routine.

- Devise strategies to help you deal with your cravings, these will also help you stay smoke free. There are non-nicotine prescription medicines that your doctor may consider to help reduce your cravings. For example, NRT can also help reduce your cravings. Some people find that sipping on ice-cold water helps with cravings, also relaxation and breathing exercises will be of help.

- Remind yourself of the benefits of quitting smoking and why you are quitting. Keep in mind that your body begins to heal 20 minutes after you stop smoking and on top of that you will also be saving money!

- Accept that you may feel short-tempered at times, take this as a sign that your body is getting rid of the poison and remind yourself that this time will pass.
- Reward yourself at every milestone however small, after a smoke-free week, 2 weeks, a month and so forth. Celebrate these achievements with the money you have saved from not buying cigarettes. Treat yourself!

And last but not least a piece of advice. If you relapse, don't panic, its not all doom and gloom and don't give up just because you've made a mistake and had a cigarette or two. Many people stumble before they give up for good. Do not treat your relapse as a failure or an excuse to give up, see this as a challenge and an opportunity to learn from this experience. They say experience is a great teacher so use this experience as a learning curve and work out why you smoked again, which formulas worked for you and which didn't work and the changes you need to make in your next attempt. After gathering all the information you should then try again whenever you are ready.

Points to consider

- If you relapse find out why you slipped and make plans for how you can avoid getting in the same situation next time and put measures in place in case it happens next time.
- Take the slip as a temporary set back and pick yourself up don't view it as a failure.

- Seek support from a reliable and trustworthy source as soon as you relapse.
- Get through your list of reasons for quitting and remind yourself why you are doing it then get yourself back on track.
- Look into other quit smoking options which you hadn't considered before. Sometimes it's a case of trial and error until you find what works for you.
- Be kind to yourself, forgive yourself and accept that you have made a mistake and start again on a clean slate. After all one of the secrets of success is to refuse to let temporary setbacks defeat us.

**

Book References

Paul Gilbert, Overcoming Depression. A Self-Help Guide Using Cognitive Behavioural Techniques (Robinson Publishing Ltd, 1997)

Alice Muir, Overcome Depression (Hodder & Stoughton Ltd, 2013)

Keith Souter, Understanding and Dealing with Depression (Summersdale Publishers Ltd, 2013)

Neel Burton, Growing From Depression (Acheron Press, 2010)

Josie Hardley and Carol Staudacher, Hypnosis For Change (MJF Books, 1996)

Costas Papageorgiou, Hannah Goring and Justin Haslam, Coping With Depression. A Guide to What Works For Patients, Carers and Professionals (One World Publications, 2011)

Terry Louker and Olga Gregson, Manage Your Stress for a Happier Life (The McGraw-Hill Companies, 1997)

Xandria Williams, Stress. Recognize and Resolve. How to Free Yourself from Stress Whatever Your Circumstances (Charles Letts & Co Ltd, 1993)

**

Resources

www.nosmokingday.org.uk
Part of the British Heart Foundation website

www.nhs.uk/smokefree
The main NHS stop smoking website

www.ash.org.uk
ASH is a campaigning public health charity that works to eliminate the harm caused by tobacco.

https://www.nhs.uk/smokefree/help-and-advice/e-cigarettes
NHS Smokefree website gives information about e-cigarettes

www.quitsmokingsupport.com
Provides advice and support to help people stop smoking

whyquit.com
Website offering advice and support for those who wish to give up smoking

quitsmokingonline.com
Offers advice and support to those wishing to give up smoking

quitnet.meyouhealth.com
Quitnet has been helping smokers quit since 1995, and it's still going strong! It's the safe, supportive place where smokers and ex-smokers gather to quit and stay quit.

www.myumc/treatments/cognitivebehaviourtherapy
my Virtual medical Centre offering education around
Cognitive behavioural therapy

www.simplypsychology.org
Offers articles on different psychology

www.hypnotherapy-directory.org.uk
Website offering advice and support in the area of
hypnotherapy

www.who.int>mediacentre>factsheets
Website of the World health Organisation

**

Index

Acrolein, 4, 25
Acupuncture, 7, 91
Addiction, 5, 29, 39
Addictive behaviours, 30
Adrenal glands, 40
Advertising, 35
Age related Macular Degeneration, 44
Allergies, 17
Ammonia, 4, 25
Anger, 41
Appetite, 34, 41, 102, 103, 107
Arsenic, 4, 24
Arteries, 23
Asthma, 17, 44

Babies, 17, 126
Bad breath, 20
Belief, 61
Blindness, 44
Boredom, 5, 33
brainwashed mind, 6, 63
Breast milk production, 18
Breathing awareness, 88
Breathing Exercise, 7, 89
Breathing problems, 45
British Association For Behavioural and Cognitive Therapists (BABCP), 82
British Psychological Society (BPS), 82

Cancer Research UK, 20
Cancers, 43

Carbon-dioxide, 88
Carbon-monoxide, 23, 27
Cardiovascular system, 43
Central nervous system, 43
Champix, 7, 101, 102
Children, 17, 18, 20, 21, 31, 42, 44, 45, 47, 81
Chinese medicine, 91
Chronic bronchitis, 24, 46
Cognitive Behavioural Therapy, 6, 12, 79
Cognitive Dissonance, 6, 52
Confusion, 24
Cortisol, 40
Cot death, 17, 19
Counselling, 7, 82, 89

Deep Breathing Technique, 7, 88
Denial, 10, 23, 35, 53
Diabetes, 44
Diet, 7, 12, 34, 105, 106
Digestive system, 43
Dizziness, 97, 98, 102, 103

E-Cigarettes, 4, 26
Emphysema, 24, 44
Exercise, 8, 107

Fear, 65
Fertility problems, 44
Food, 15, 34, 42, 47, 73, 78, 87, 105, 106
Formaldehyde, 4, 25

Gum, 95, 98

Headaches, 95, 96, 98, 99, 102, 103
Heart attacks, 23
Heart defects, 17
Heart disease, 18, 24, 45, 46
Herbicides, 24
Hydrogen Cyanide, 24
Hypnosis, 6, 61, 67, 68, 69, 70, 90
Hypnotherapist, 68
Hypnotherapy, 6, 67, 68

Illnesses, 35, 36, 43, 45
Inhaler, 7, 97
Irritability, 41, 42
IVF, 18

Longevity, 5, 46
Low blood pressure, 24
Lung cancer, 18, 24, 45, 46, 48
Lung infections, 17

Medications, 12, 101
Meditation, 59, 90
Mental illness, 35
Miscarriage, 44
Motivation, 6, 55
Motivational interviewing, 83, 84

Naphthylamine, 4, 25
Nausea, 24
Nicotiana tabacum, 26
Nicotine Chewing Gum, 7, 95
Nicotine Lozenges, 7, 98
Nicotine Mouth Spray, 7, 98

Nicotine Nasal Spray, 7, 96
Nicotine Replacement Therapy, 7, 93
Nitrogen-dioxide, 4, 25
Nitrosamines, 25

Parental influence, 31
Patches, 41, 93, 94
Peer pressure, 5, 31
Pesticides, 24
Pets, 5, 44
Positive thinking, 63, 85
Pregnancy, 17, 126
Premature ageing, 44
Premature birth, 44
Premature death, 15
Progressive Muscle Relaxation(PMR), 7, 89
Psychoactive substance, 39

Relapse, 6, 51, 52
Reproductive system, 43
Respiratory problems, 17
Respiratory system, 43
Rheumatoid arthritis, 44
Royal College of Physicians, 39

Second hand smoke, 15, 21, 31, 45
Self-efficacy, 6, 53, 54
Smoking in pregnancy, 16, 19
Snacking, 34
Social smokers, 35
Social support, 82
Sore throat, 102
Sprays, 41, 93, 94, 98

Stages of Change Model (SCM), 49
Stress, 5, 16, 32, 40, 42, 52, 64, 66, 68, 78, 81, 88, 89, 107, 111
Strokes, 23
Subconscious mind, 30, 61, 62, 63, 65, 68, 71, 76, 86, 112
Sudden Infant Death Syndrome(SIDS), 17
Suggestion therapy, 67

Tar, 23, 27
Taste buds, 33, 34, 73, 106
Teenagers, 32, 35, 64
The mind, 12, 61, 68
Tobacco industry, 36
Tobacco manufacturers, 63, 65
Tolerance, 39, 40

Vapour, 26, 27, 97
Vomiting, 24, 99, 103

Weight loss, 33
Will-power, 6, 54
Withdrawal symptoms, 34, 40, 41, 42, 65, 66, 68, 81, 88, 89, 90, 91, 93, 94, 95, 96, 101, 103, 107
World Health Organisation, 15

Yoga,, 59, 90

Zyban, 7, 101, 102

**

Appendix

1- What's in a smoke
2- The nicotine cycle
3- Effects of smoking on babies- in pregnancy
4- Long term health effects of smoking tobacco
5- Smoking lungs
6- When you stop smoking
7- The cycle of change
8- Stars- 2 pages

What's in a Smoke

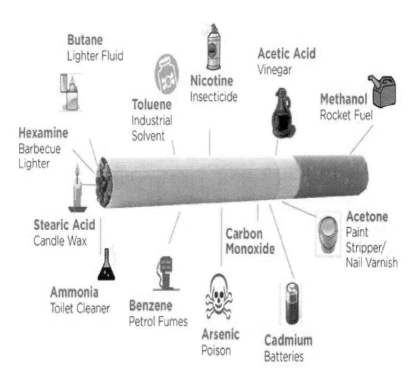

The Nicotine Cycle

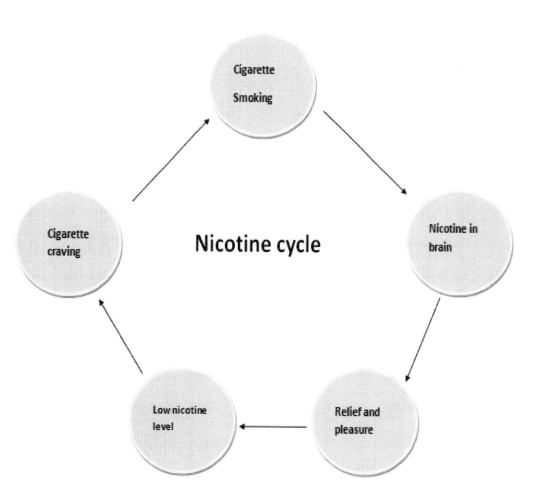

Effects on Babies in Pregnancy

Effects on babies

- Smoking during pregnancy may cause health problems in babies, like –
  - Low birth weight
  - Premature birth (being born too early)
  - Still birth
  - Respiratory complications
  - Congenital heart defects
  - CNS effects
  - Fetal death
  - Infant death

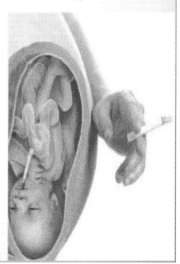

Long Term Health Effects of Smoking Tobacco

The Long Term Health Effects Of Smoking Tobacco

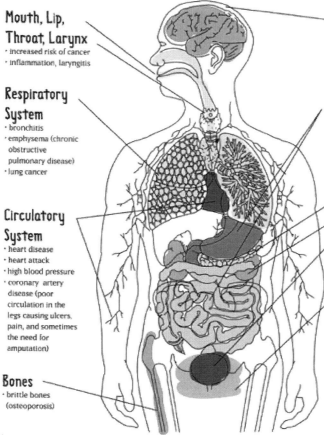

Mouth, Lip, Throat, Larynx
- increased risk of cancer
- inflammation, laryngitis

Respiratory System
- bronchitis
- emphysema (chronic obstructive pulmonary disease)
- lung cancer

Circulatory System
- heart disease
- heart attack
- high blood pressure
- coronary artery disease (poor circulation in the legs causing ulcers, pain, and sometimes the need for amputation)

Bones
- brittle bones (osteoporosis)

Immune System
- depressed immune response
- increased infections

Brain
- increased risk of brain hemorrhage (stroke)
- women using contraceptive pill have an even greater risk of stroke

Stomach and Intestines
- lining becomes tender
- bleeding
- ulcers, slow to heal
- may lead to cancer

Pancreas, Kidney and Bladder
- increased risk of cancer

Reproductive System Male and Female
- decreased sperm count and movement
- lowered sex drive
- egg damage, irregular menstrual cycle and altered hormone levels
- cancers of the cervix, penis and anus
- early onset of menopause
- increased risk of breast cancer

Pregnancy and Babies
- lower than average birth weight
- high risk of Sudden Infant Death Syndrome
- increased risk of premature birth
- higher increased risk of miscarriage and still births
- increased risk of impairment in mental and physical development
- nicotine carried to baby in breast milk

Smoking Lungs

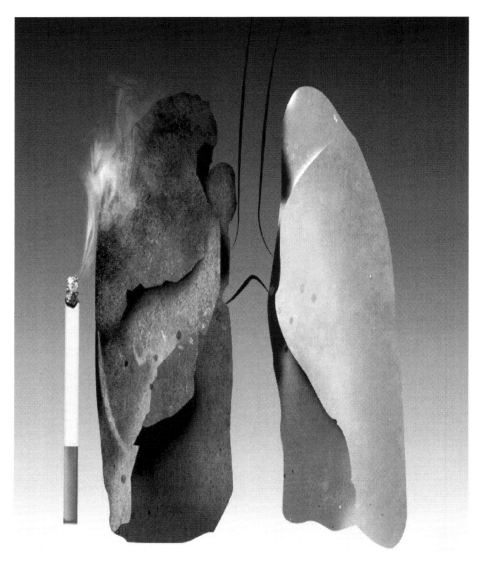

When You Stop Smoking

When smokers stop smoking:

Within 20 minutes of smoking the cigarette, body starts repairing itself, which continue for years. All benefits are lost by smoking just one cigarette a day (according to the American Cancer Society).

20 minutes

- Blood pressure drops to normal
- Pulse rate drops to normal
- Body temperature of hands and feet increase to normal

8 hours

- Carbon monoxide level in blood drops to normal
- Oxygen level in blood increases to normal

24 hours

- Chance of heart attack decreases

48 hours

- Nerve ending start regrowing
- Ability to smell and taste enhanced

1 to 9 months

- Coughing, sinus congestion, fatigue and shortness of breath decrease
- Cilia regrow in lungs increasing ability to handle mucus, clean the lungs, reduce infection
- Body's overall energy increases

10 years

- Lung cancer deathe rate similar to that of nonsmokers
- Precancerous cells are replaced
- Risk of cancer of the mouth, throat, esophagus, bladder, kidney and pancreas decrease

15 years

- Risk of coronary heart disease reduce to nonsmoker's level

2 weeks to 3 months

- Circulation improves
- Walking becomes easier
- Lung function increases up to 30%

1 year

- Excess risk of coronary heart disease reduces to 50%

5 years

- Lung cancer death rate for average former smoker (one pack a day) decreases by almost half
- Stroke risk is reduced to that of a non smoker 5-15 years after quiting
- Risk of cancer of the mouth, throat and esophagus is half that of a smoker's

The Cycle of Change

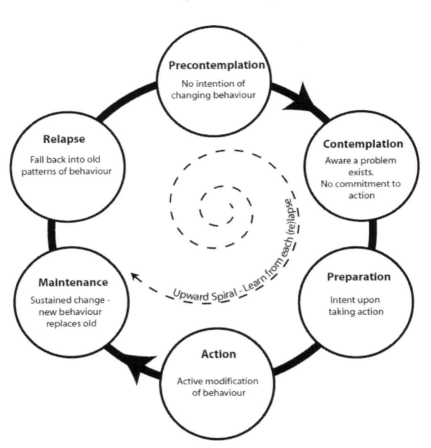

Stars

Stars

Other books by Josephine Spire

UNDERSTANDING AND MANAGING DEPRESSION AND STRESS
ISBN 978-1-84716-685-2 £9.99

Depression is a traumatic and cruel illness which affects over 150 million people worldwide. It can affect anyone regardless of their age, gender, race or status. However, depression is like any other illness, it has to be dealt with and not ignored.

In addition, **stress** affects our minds, bodies and relationships and most of us encounter stressful experiences in our lives but the difference is that we all cope differently. Some people are better at dealing with their stress whereas other people find it a struggle to navigate through it. Throughout this book the reader will learn various mind-techniques and coping skills that can be practiced as part of a self-help strategy to overcome depression and stress.

SELF HYPNOSIS AND POSITIVE AFFIRMATIONS
THE ART OF SELF THERAPY
ISBN 978-1-84716-499-5 £9.99

Hypnosis is the gentle healer, no chemicals, no side effects and it puts the patient in a state that holds great potential for healing by giving the patient access to the subconscious mind. Self- Hypnosis and Positive Affirmations is a book about how hypnosis combined with positive affirmations can be powerful in treating a number of physical, psychological, stress related disorders, phobias and promoting sporting performance among others. This book is original and practical and will benefit anyone who wishes to investigate further. More and more people are beginning to realise and appreciate the healing power of hypnosis and affirmations